celebrate
Christmas

celebrate Christmas

The bumper book of festive food and craft

MURDOCH BOOKS

Contents

Christmas
Wishes

Christmas is Coming

Christmas Day countdown

THE KEY TO SUCCESS IS ORGANISATION, SO TO HELP YOU PLAN AHEAD AND SAVE TIME AND WORRY, HERE'S A SCHEDULE TO GUIDE YOU THROUGH THE DAYS AND MONTHS LEADING UP TO CHRISTMAS DAY.

ONE YEAR AHEAD

✶ Of course, it sounds ridiculous to start planning this early, but it's worth having a look at the post-Christmas sales. This is an ideal time to stock up on budget-priced wrapping paper, cards and Christmas decorations and to start gathering ideas for your next Christmas bash.

SIX TO THREE MONTHS AHEAD

- ✶ It's time to work out your budget, a rough guest list and plan your menu.
- ✶ If you need to hire equipment—anything from a marquee to cutlery—do so.
- ✶ Christmas cakes and puddings can be made well ahead of time if they are stored properly. Wrap them securely in greaseproof paper, then in plastic wrap and store in an airtight container in the refrigerator or a cool, dark place. A long storage time is actually beneficial as it allows the flavours to develop. As a general rule, Christmas cakes can be stored for up to 3 months and puddings for up to 6 weeks. Both can also be frozen for up to 12 months.
- ✶ Make your liqueur fruits so they are ready for Christmas Day or for giving as gifts (see pages 172–173). If you can, buy fruits in season when they are cheaper and full of flavour. Bottled liqueur fruits will keep for up to 6 months.

ONE MONTH AHEAD

- ✶ If you have ample storage space, purchase wine, beer and soft drinks now. Or, if you have planned a large party, order drinks now and arrange to have them delivered a few days ahead of the party.
- ✶ Order turkeys and hams. As a general guide, a 7 kg (16 lb) ham will serve around 20 people and a 4.5 kg (10 lb 2 oz) turkey will feed 6–8 people when served as a main course with vegetables and all the trimmings.
- ✶ Make your mincemeat (fruit mince) for mince pies as it takes about a month to mature (see page 188).
- ✶ Start thinking about and making your table decorations.
- ✶ Think about and plan your table settings.
- ✶ Make jams (jellies), pickles and chutneys for stocking your pantry and for gifts (see page 214 for methods of sterilising jars).

Christmas is coming,
The geese are getting fat,
Please to put a penny
In the old man's hat.

19
13
24
17
5
14
21
11
23
16
20
22
18
15
12

* For those who like their cake a little on the tipsy side, make the cake at least a few weeks ahead, and then once a week prick the top of the cake with a very thin cake skewer and carefully spoon or brush over a little alcohol of your choice (usually brandy), letting it soak in. Make sure you wrap the cake well each time so it stays moist.

* If you are planning to make a boiled pudding, don't forget to buy some calico and string (or the correct-sized steamer basin) and make sure you have a pot large enough to boil the pudding in.

* Christmas cakes and puddings make great gifts, and look wonderful when packaged either with colourful wrappings or simply some brown paper, straw or raffia and a couple of holly leaves.

PREPARING FOR YOUR CHRISTMAS FEAST

* Check that you have enough crockery, glassware and cutlery for the number of people you are expecting, allowing a few spares. Hiring can be inexpensive if you shop around to get the most competitive rate. Alternatively, borrow from friends or family—mix-and-match crockery can look wonderful!

* If your attempts to roast a turkey or bake a ham are a one-off, buy disposable foil baking dishes from supermarkets. Use two foil dishes together (one inside the other) to give a stronger base under the weight of your turkey or ham.

* Make sure you have a portable insulated food cooler, which will conveniently keep food hot or cold. Put the cooked ham, turkey or other large joint in the cooler, loosely covered, while you finish the vegetables and gravy.

SHOPPING

- Order turkeys and hams and other unusual food items well ahead so you don't miss out.
- Buy non-perishable foods early on to avoid frustrating delays at the supermarket. Make detailed shopping lists and delegate if possible. Don't turn down offers of help!
- Buy wine, sparkling wine and soft drinks well ahead, keeping an eye out for specials in the days and weeks leading up to Christmas.

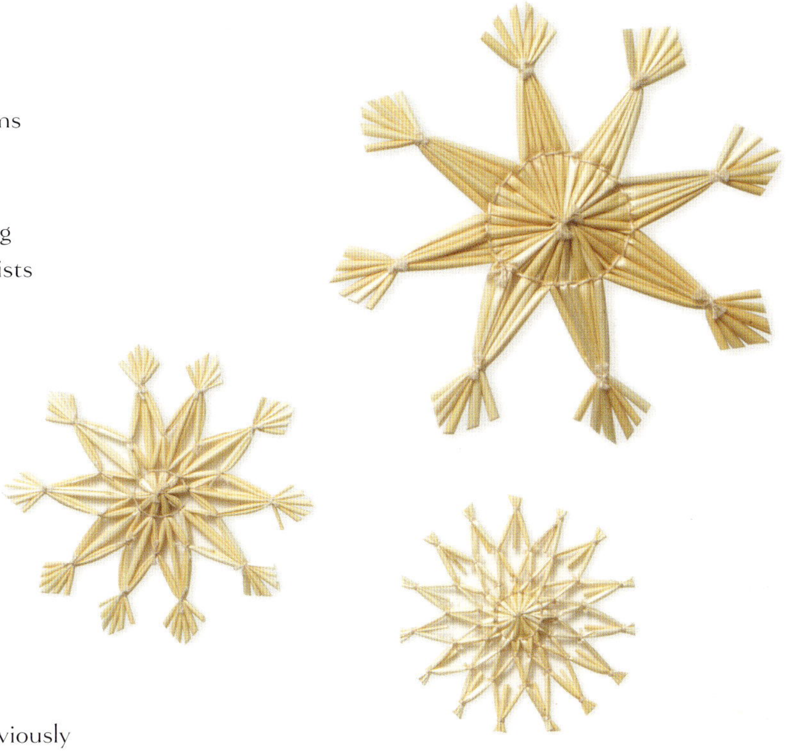

STORAGE

- You will need plenty of fridge space for a large turkey or ham. This may require removing a shelf and some organisation to fit everything, and obviously you want to have this worked out before the kitchen frenzy on Christmas Day.
- If you are really pushed for space for storing food, think about hiring a fridge or freezer for the festive season.
- Think about what else you need to be cooking in the oven at the same time as your roast. For example, how are you going to fit the roast vegetables in the oven if they are being served alongside the ham? A covered kettle barbecue is ideal for cooking hams, allowing you a lot more space in your oven on the day. And bear in mind that the ham and turkey will keep hot for quite a while once removed from the oven.
- Don't leave foods unrefrigerated for too long in warmer climates or heated rooms. Room temperature is the perfect environment for bacteria to breed, and this can cause food poisoning, especially in chicken, duck and turkey.

LEFTOVERS

- Don't worry if you have leftovers—you don't have to eat ham sandwiches for a week! Turkey and ham leftovers can easily be turned into a variety of tasty dishes (see pages 112–115).
- Freeze your leftover ham bone and cooked or uncooked (after boning) turkey bones for later in the year. Make split pea and ham soup with the ham bone and make delicious stock from the turkey bones.
- Freeze suitable leftovers in quantities for one or two people. Smaller portions defrost more quickly than large blocks. They will be very welcome when it's time to relax.

'Twas the night before Christmas,
when all through the house
Not a creature was stirring,
not even a mouse ...'

Drinks and Nibbles

Berry and cherry punch

SERVES 10

- 1 lemon
- 425 g (15 oz) tinned pitted black cherries
- 125 g (4½ oz) halved strawberries
- 600 g (1 lb 5 oz) assorted fresh or frozen berries
- 500 ml (17 fl oz/2 cups) lemonade
- 750 ml (26 fl oz/3 cups) ginger ale
- 250 ml (9 fl oz/1 cup) cold black tea
- 10 torn mint leaves
- ice cubes, to serve

Peel the skin from the lemon with a vegetable peeler, avoiding the bitter white pith. Cut into long thin strips.

Drain the black cherries and put in a large bowl. Add the strawberries, berries, lemonade, ginger ale, tea, mint leaves and the lemon zest. Cover and chill for at least 3 hours. Add ice cubes when serving.

Mulled wine

SERVES 6

- 12 cloves
- 2 oranges
- 3 tablespoons sugar
- 1 whole nutmeg, grated
- 4 cinnamon sticks
- 2 lemons, thinly sliced
- 750 ml (24 fl oz/3 cups) full-bodied red wine

Push the cloves into the oranges and place in a saucepan with the sugar, nutmeg, cinnamon sticks and lemon. Pour in 500 ml (17 fl oz/2 cups) water and bring to the boil, then reduce the heat, cover the pan and simmer for 20 minutes. Allow to cool, then strain and discard the fruit and spices.

Pour the mixture into a saucepan, add the full bodied red wine and heat until almost boiling—do not allow to boil or the alcohol will evaporate off. Serve in heatproof glasses.

Sangria

SERVES 6

2 tablespoons caster (superfine) sugar
1 tablespoon lemon juice
1 tablespoon orange juice
1 orange, thinly sliced
1 lemon, thinly sliced
1 lime, thinly sliced
750 ml (26 fl oz/3 cups) chilled red wine
ice cubes, to serve

Mix the caster sugar with the lemon and orange juice in a large bowl until the sugar has dissolved. Add the fruit slices to the bowl with the red wine and plenty of ice. Stir well until very cold. Serve in large wine glasses. (Do not strain.)

NOTES: This traditional Spanish drink can be made in large quantities, and its flavour will improve over several hours—it can be made up to a day in advance. Chopped seasonal fruit, such as peaches, pears and pineapples, can be added to this basic recipe. Good-quality wine is not essential in sangria, so use a table wine or even a cask wine.

Buttered rum

SERVES 4

1 tablespoon sugar
250 ml (9 fl oz/1 cup) rum
1–2 teaspoons softened unsalted butter

Put the sugar, rum and 500 ml (17 fl oz/2 cups) boiling water in a heatproof jug. Stir to dissolve the sugar, then divide the rum among four mugs.

Stir the butter into each mug and serve.

Chicken liver and Grand Marnier pâté

- SERVES 8
- PREPARATION TIME 20 minutes plus chilling and setting
- COOKING TIME 10 minutes

750 g (1 lb 10 oz) chicken livers, well trimmed
250 ml (9 fl oz/1 cup) milk
200 g (7 oz) butter, softened
4 spring onions (scallions), finely chopped
1 tablespoon Grand Marnier
1 tablespoon orange juice concentrate
½ orange, very thinly sliced

JELLIED LAYER
1 tablespoon orange juice concentrate
1 tablespoon Grand Marnier
315 ml (10¾ fl oz/1¼ cups) canned chicken consommé, undiluted
2½ teaspoons powdered gelatine

Put the trimmed chicken livers in a bowl, add the milk and stir to combine. Cover and refrigerate for 1 hour. Drain the livers and discard the milk. Rinse in cold water, drain and pat dry with paper towels.

Melt one-third of the butter in a frying pan, add the chopped spring onion and cook for 2–3 minutes, or until tender, but not brown. Add the livers and cook, stirring, over medium heat for 4–5 minutes, or until just cooked. Remove from the heat and cool a little.

Transfer the livers to a food processor and process until very smooth. Chop the remaining butter, add to the food processor with the Grand Marnier and orange juice concentrate and process until creamy. Season, to taste, with salt and freshly ground black pepper. Transfer to a 1.25 litre (44 fl oz/5 cup) serving dish, cover the surface with plastic wrap and chill for 1½ hours, or until firm.

For the jellied layer, whisk together the orange juice concentrate, Grand Marnier and 125 ml (4 fl oz/½ cup) of the consommé. Sprinkle the gelatine over the liquid in an even layer and leave until the gelatine is spongy — do not stir. Heat the remaining consommé in a saucepan, remove from the heat and add the gelatine mixture. Stir to dissolve the gelatine, then leave to cool and thicken to the consistency of raw egg white, but not set.

Press the orange slices lightly into the surface of the pâté and spoon the thickened jelly evenly over the top. Refrigerate until set. Serve at room temperature with toast or crackers.

NOTE: Grand Marnier is a cognac-based liqueur with an orange flavour.

Sweet onion tarts

MAKES 20 PREPARATION TIME 30 minutes plus chilling
COOKING TIME 45 minutes

PASTRY

125 g (4½ oz/1 cup) plain (all-purpose) flour
80 g (2¾ oz) butter, chopped
1 tablespoon bottled green peppercorns, drained
1 egg yolk
1 teaspoon dijon mustard
2 teaspoons iced water

SWEET ONION FILLING

2 tablespoons olive oil
3 onions, sliced
1 garlic clove, sliced
2 teaspoons sugar
2 tablespoons balsamic vinegar
40 g (1½ oz/⅓ cup) raisins

1 tablespoon olive paste
80 g (2¾ oz) feta cheese

Lightly grease 20 holes in two 12-hole patty pans or mini muffin tins. Sift the flour and ¼ teaspoon salt into a bowl. Using your fingertips, rub in the butter until the mixture resembles fine breadcrumbs. Make a well in the centre. Crush the peppercorns with the back of a knife and chop finely. Add to the flour with the egg yolk, mustard and the iced water. Mix with a flat-bladed knife, using a cutting action, until the mixture comes together in beads. Turn onto a lightly floured surface and press into a ball. Wrap in plastic wrap and refrigerate for 20 minutes.

Preheat the oven to 200°C (400°F/Gas 6). Roll out the dough on a lightly floured surface to 2–3 mm (1/16–⅛ inch). Cut 20 rounds with an 8 cm (3¼ inch) cutter. Put in the patty pans and prick with a fork. Bake for 8–10 minutes, or until golden.

To make the filling, heat the oil in a heavy-based saucepan. Add the onion and garlic and cook, covered, over low heat for 30 minutes, or until the onion is very soft and beginning to brown. Increase the heat to moderate, add the sugar and vinegar and cook, stirring, until most of the liquid has evaporated and the onion is glossy. Stir in the raisins.

Spread a little olive paste in the base of each pastry case. Spoon the onion mixture over the olive paste and crumble the feta on top. Serve warm or at room temperature.

Smoked salmon tartlets

MAKES 24 PREPARATION TIME 30 minutes plus chilling
COOKING TIME 30 minutes

250 g (9 oz) cream cheese, at room temperature
1½ tablespoons wholegrain mustard
2 teaspoons dijon mustard
2 tablespoons lemon juice
2 tablespoons chopped dill
6 sheets ready-rolled puff pastry
300 g (10½ oz) smoked salmon, cut into thin strips
2 tablespoons capers, drained
dill sprigs, to garnish

Preheat the oven to 210°C (415°F/Gas 6–7) Line two large baking trays with baking paper.

Mix the cream cheese, mustards, lemon juice and dill in a bowl, then cover and refrigerate.

Cut four 9.5 cm (3¾ inch) rounds from each sheet of pastry, using a fluted cutter, and place on the baking trays. Prick the pastries all over. Cover and refrigerate for 10 minutes.

Bake the pastries in batches for 7 minutes, then remove from the oven and use a spoon to flatten the centre of each pastry. Return to the oven and bake for a further 5 minutes, or until the pastry is golden. Allow to cool.

Spread some of the cream cheese mixture over each pastry round, leaving a 1 cm (½ inch) border. Arrange the salmon over the top. Decorate with a few capers and a sprig of dill. Serve immediately.

CHRISTMAS CARDS

Sending greeting cards at Christmas did not become popular until the 1870s. In the eighteenth century, in some places, Valentine and New Year cards were exchanged and in Britain, children made cards at school with a Christmas greeting for their parents. In the early 1840s, Sir Henry Cole, an English businessman (interested in art) is said to have come up with the idea of producing a printed Christmas greeting card. An artist did a design and Sir Henry produced one thousand cards to sell. Although the idea didn't take off straight away, later in the century advances in the printing process and cheaper postage allowed the idea to gradually spread worldwide.

TO MAKE YOUR OWN CARDS

Ribbons, buttons, scraps of fabric, paper of various kinds and card of different weights are the bare ingredients of cardmaking. The main necessities, though, are a little creativity and a big sense of fun. Cards such as the two shown here are easy to make and a pleasure to receive.

Puff pastry twists

MAKES 96 PREPARATION TIME 10 minutes
COOKING TIME 10 minutes per batch

- 2 sheets ready-rolled puff pastry, thawed
- 1 egg, lightly beaten
- 80 g (2¾ oz/½ cup) sesame seeds, poppy seeds or caraway seeds

Preheat the oven to 200°C (400°F/Gas 6). Lightly grease two baking trays. Brush the pastry with the egg and sprinkle with the sesame seeds.

Cut the pastry in half and then into 1 cm (½ inch) wide strips. Twist the strips and place on the greased baking trays. Bake each batch for about 10 minutes, or until golden brown.

NOTE: Store the twists in an airtight container for up to a week. Refresh in a 180°C (350°F/Gas 4) oven for 2–3 minutes, then allow to cool.

Parmesan and thyme wafers

MAKES 18 PREPARATION TIME 5 minutes
COOKING TIME 10 minutes per batch

- 125 g (4½ oz/1¼ cups) finely grated parmesan cheese
- 3 teaspoons thyme leaves

Preheat the oven to 180°C (350°F/Gas 4). Line two baking trays with baking paper. Combine the parmesan and thyme in a bowl.

Place 2 tablespoons of the mixture on the prepared trays and shape into rough rectangles.

Bake for 8–10 minutes, or until light golden. Cool the wafers on the trays, then break into smaller pieces.

Grissini wrapped in smoked salmon

MAKES 24 PREPARATION TIME 20 minutes
COOKING TIME nil

125 g (4½ oz) cream cheese, at room temperature
1–2 tablespoons chopped dill
¼ teaspoon finely grated lemon zest
24 ready-made grissini
8–10 slices smoked salmon, cut into thin strips

Mix the cream cheese, chopped dill and lemon zest in a bowl until the dill is well distributed. Season, to taste, with salt.

Spread the cream cheese mixture over half of each grissini. Wrap some of the smoked salmon around each grissini, over the cream cheese, securing it with more cream cheese.

NOTE: Prepare these grissini close to serving (up to about 30 minutes before) as the biscuits will start to soften once the cheese is spread on them.

Cucumber rounds with avocado and turkey

MAKES 30 PREPARATION TIME 20 minutes
COOKING TIME nil

3 Lebanese (short) cucumbers
100 g (3½ oz) sliced smoked turkey
½ avocado, mashed
1 garlic clove, crushed
2 tablespoons cranberry sauce
2 tablespoons sour cream
cranberry sauce, extra, to garnish
alfalfa sprouts or mustard cress, to garnish

Slice the cucumbers into 1.5 cm (5/8 inch) rounds to make 30 pieces. Cut 30 rounds from the turkey using a 3 cm (1¼ inch) cutter.

Combine the avocado with the garlic, cranberry sauce and sour cream. Spoon 1 teaspoon onto each cucumber round and top with a round of turkey. Spoon a little of the extra cranberry sauce on top and garnish with alfalfa sprouts.

'I will honour Christmas in my heart,
and try to keep it all the year.'

CHARLES DICKENS

Tomato and haloumi skewers

MAKES 22 PREPARATION TIME 30 minutes
COOKING TIME 10 minutes

500 g (1 lb 2 oz) haloumi cheese
5 large handfuls basil
150 g (5½ oz) semi-dried (sun-blushed) tomatoes
2 tablespoons balsamic vinegar
2 tablespoons extra virgin olive oil
1 teaspoon sea salt

Preheat a barbecue hotplate or chargrill pan. Cut the cheese into 1.5 cm (5/8 inch) pieces. Thread a basil leaf onto a small skewer, followed by a piece of haloumi, a semi-dried tomato, another basil leaf and another piece of haloumi. Finish with a basil leaf. Repeat to use the remaining ingredients.

Place the skewers on the barbecue hotplate and cook, turning occasionally until the cheese is golden brown, brushing with the combined vinegar and oil while cooking. Sprinkle with the salt and serve hot or warm.

NOTES: To make semi-dried (sun-blushed) tomatoes, cut ripe roma (plum) tomatoes into quarters and place them on a wire rack. Sit the rack on a baking tray. Lightly sprinkle the tomatoes with salt, pepper and a pinch of sugar. Bake in a preheated 160°C (315°F/Gas 2–3) oven for 3–4 hours, until dry but still soft. The drying time will depend on the amount of moisture and the size of the tomatoes. Keep in an airtight container in the refrigerator for 4–5 days. Drizzle with olive oil, if desired.

Cranberry and apple martini

SERVES 6

3 tablespoons dry vermouth
crushed ice
270 ml (9½ fl oz) cloudy apple juice
185 ml (6 fl oz/¾ cup) gin
1½ tablespoons apple schnapps
90 ml (3 fl oz) cranberry juice
6 apple slices, such as royal gala, to serve

For the best result, mix one cocktail at a time. Pour 2 teaspoons of vermouth into a chilled martini glass and swirl to coat the sides. Discard the remaining liquid.

Half fill a cocktail shaker with the crushed ice, add 45 ml (1½ fl oz) of apple juice, 2½ tablespoons of gin, 1 teaspoon of apple schnapps and 3 teaspoons of cranberry juice. Stir and strain into the glass and garnish with a slice of apple. Repeat to make six martinis.

Blood orange Champagne cocktail

SERVES 4

125 ml (4 fl oz/½ cup) Campari
125 ml (4 fl oz/½ cup) blood orange juice
Champagne or sparkling white wine

Divide the Campari and orange juice among four cocktail glasses. Top with Champagne or sparkling wine and serve.

Eggnog

SERVES 6–8

4 eggs, separated
90 g (3¼ oz/⅓ cup) caster (superfine) sugar
315 ml (10¾ fl oz/1¼ cups) hot milk
125 ml (4 fl oz/½ cup) bourbon
125 ml (4 fl oz/½ cup) cream
grated nutmeg, for sprinkling

Beat the egg yolks and caster sugar in a heatproof bowl until light and fluffy. Add the hot milk and stir to combine.

Bring a saucepan of water to the boil, then reduce the heat until simmering. Place the bowl over the simmering water and stir with a wooden spoon for about 5–10 minutes, or until the mixture thickens and lightly coats the back of the spoon. Remove from the heat and allow to cool.

Stir in the bourbon. Beat the cream and the four egg whites in separate bowls until soft peaks form. Fold the cream, then the egg whites into the bourbon in two batches. Pour into glasses and sprinkle with grated nutmeg.

Brandy Alexander punch

SERVES 16

750 ml (26 fl oz/3 cups) brandy
375 ml (13 fl oz/1½ cups) crème de cacao (coffee liqueur)
1.75 litres (60 fl oz/7 cups) cream
ice cubes, to serve
grated nutmeg, for sprinkling
strawberries, to garnish

Pour the brandy, crème de cacao and cream into a large bowl. Whisk to just combine. Add ice cubes to a 3.5 litre (118 fl oz/14 cup) punch bowl and pour in the brandy mixture. Sprinkle with grated nutmeg, then serve in cocktail glasses garnished with strawberry halves.

Tomato and haloumi skewers

MAKES 22 PREPARATION TIME 30 minutes
COOKING TIME 10 minutes

- 500 g (1 lb 2 oz) haloumi cheese
- 5 large handfuls basil
- 150 g (5½ oz) semi-dried (sun-blushed) tomatoes
- 2 tablespoons balsamic vinegar
- 2 tablespoons extra virgin olive oil
- 1 teaspoon sea salt

Preheat a barbecue hotplate or chargrill pan. Cut the cheese into 1.5 cm (5/8 inch) pieces. Thread a basil leaf onto a small skewer, followed by a piece of haloumi, a semi-dried tomato, another basil leaf and another piece of haloumi. Finish with a basil leaf. Repeat to use the remaining ingredients.

Place the skewers on the barbecue hotplate and cook, turning occasionally until the cheese is golden brown, brushing with the combined vinegar and oil while cooking. Sprinkle with the salt and serve hot or warm.

NOTES: To make semi-dried (sun-blushed) tomatoes, cut ripe roma (plum) tomatoes into quarters and place them on a wire rack. Sit the rack on a baking tray. Lightly sprinkle the tomatoes with salt, pepper and a pinch of sugar. Bake in a preheated 160°C (315°F/Gas 2–3) oven for 3–4 hours, until dry but still soft. The drying time will depend on the amount of moisture and the size of the tomatoes. Keep in an airtight container in the refrigerator for 4–5 days. Drizzle with olive oil, if desired.

Spicy nuts

SERVES 6 PREPARATION TIME 10 minutes
COOKING TIME 20 minutes

- 2 tablespoons olive oil
- 1/2 teaspoon ground cumin
- 1/2 teaspoon ground coriander
- 1/2 teaspoon garlic powder
- 1/4 teaspoon chilli powder
- 1/4 teaspoon ground ginger
- 1/4 teaspoon ground cinnamon
- 65 g (2 1/4 oz/2/3 cup) pecans
- 100 g (3 1/2 oz/2/3 cup) raw cashew nuts
- 240 g (8 1/2 oz/1 1/2 cups) raw almonds

Preheat the oven to 150°C (300°F/Gas 2). Heat the oil over low heat in a large frying pan and stir in the spices for 2 minutes, or until fragrant. Remove from the heat, add the nuts and stir with a wooden spoon until the nuts are well coated. Spread over a baking tray and bake for 15 minutes, or until golden. Sprinkle with salt and cool.

Devils and angels on horseback

MAKES 24 PREPARATION TIME 10 minutes
COOKING TIME 6 minutes

- 4–6 bacon slices
- 12 pitted prunes
- 12 oysters, fresh or bottled
- 2 tablespoons worcestershire sauce
- Tabasco sauce, to taste

Soak 24 toothpicks in cold water for 30 minutes to prevent them burning. Cut each bacon slice into thin strips.

Wrap a piece of bacon around each prune and secure with a toothpick.

Remove the oysters from their shells, or drain from the bottling liquid. Sprinkle lightly with worcestershire sauce and ground black pepper, to taste. Wrap each oyster in a strip of bacon, securing with a toothpick. Preheat a lightly greased grill or barbecue flatplate. Cook the savouries, turning them occasionally, until the bacon is crisp. Serve sprinkled with a dash of Tabasco sauce.

Lemon olives with vermouth

FILLS 250 g (9 oz/1⅓ cup) jar PREPARATION TIME 5 minutes plus marinating COOKING TIME nil

- 3 tablespoons dry vermouth
- 1 tablespoon lemon juice
- 2 teaspoons shredded lemon zest
- 2 tablespoons extra virgin olive oil
- 170 g (6 oz/1 cup) Spanish green or stuffed olives

Combine the vermouth, lemon juice, lemon zest and oil. Rinse the olives and pat them dry, then add to the marinade and toss well. Cover and refrigerate overnight. Serve the olives at room temperature.

Chilli and lemon olives

FILLS 750 ml (26 fl oz/3 cup) jar PREPARATION TIME 5 minutes plus marinating COOKING TIME nil

- 500 g (1 lb 2 oz/2¾ cups) cured black olives
- 2 teaspoons finely grated lemon zest
- 2 teaspoons chopped oregano
- 3 teaspoons dried chilli flakes
- olive oil, to cover

Combine the olives, lemon zest, oregano and chilli flakes. Transfer to a 750 ml (26 fl oz/3 cup) sterilised jar, and add enough olive oil to cover. Seal, then chill in the refrigerator for at least 2 days. Return to room temperature before serving.

Herb cheese log

SERVES 12 PREPARATION TIME 25 minutes plus 3 hours refrigeration COOKING TIME nil

- 500 g (1 lb 2 oz) cream cheese, at room temperature
- 1 tablespoon lemon juice
- 1 garlic clove, crushed
- 2 teaspoons chopped thyme
- 2 teaspoons chopped tarragon
- 1 tablespoon chopped flat-leaf (Italian) parsley
- 50 g (1¾ oz/2 bunches) chives, snipped

Beat the cream cheese in a large bowl with electric beaters until soft and creamy. Mix in the lemon juice and garlic. In a separate bowl, combine the thyme, tarragon and parsley.

Line a 20 x 30 cm (8 x 12 inch) shallow tin with foil. Spread the snipped chives over the base of the tin, then dollop the cream cheese over the chives. Using a palette knife, gently join the dollops, spreading the mixture and pushing it into any gaps. Sprinkle the herbs over the cheese. Lift the foil out of the tin and place it on a flat surface. Roll into a log, starting from the longest edge, then cover and place on a baking tray.

Refrigerate the cheese log for at least 3 hours, or preferably overnight. Serve with crackers or crusty bread.

Mushroom pâté

SERVES 8–10 PREPARATION TIME 15 minutes plus 2 hours refrigeration COOKING TIME 5 minutes

- 40 g (1½ oz) butter
- 1 tablespoon oil
- 400 g (13 oz) flat mushrooms, chopped
- 2 garlic cloves, crushed
- 3 spring onions (scallions), chopped
- 1 tablespoon lemon juice
- 100 g (3½ oz) ricotta
- 100 g (3½ oz) cream cheese, at room temperature
- 2 tablespoons chopped coriander (cilantro)

Heat the butter and oil in a large frying pan over medium heat. Add the mushrooms and garlic. Cook for 5 minutes, or until the mushrooms have softened and the mushroom liquid has evaporated. Stir in the spring onion, then allow to cool.

Process the mushroom mixture with the lemon juice, ricotta, cream cheese and coriander until smooth. Season, to taste, then spoon into a serving dish. Cover and refrigerate for 2 hours to firm.

NOTE: Large flat mushrooms have more flavour than the smaller button mushrooms. Field (or wild) mushrooms can also be used.

Smoked trout dip

SERVES 4–6 PREPARATION TIME 25 minutes
COOKING TIME nil

- 250 g (8 oz) smoked rainbow trout
- 1½ teaspoons olive oil
- 125 ml (4 fl oz/½ cup) cream
- 1 tablespoon lemon juice
- pinch of cayenne pepper

Remove the skin and bones from the smoked trout. Put the flesh in a food processor or blender with the olive oil, 2 teaspoons of the cream and the lemon juice. Blend to a thick paste, then slowly add the remaining cream until well mixed. Season, to taste, with salt and the cayenne pepper. Serve with grissini or water crackers and baby radishes or other vegetables, for dipping.

NOTE: This dip can be made a few days ahead and kept, covered, in the refrigerator.

Cheese fruit log

SERVES 6 PREPARATION TIME 15 minutes plus 2–3 hours refrigeration COOKING TIME 5 minutes

- 3 tablespoons shelled pistachio nuts
- 250 g (9 oz) cream cheese, at room temperature
- 50 g (1¾ oz) dried apricots, finely chopped
- 3 spring onions (scallions), finely chopped
- 3 tablespoons sun-dried tomatoes, drained and finely chopped
- 3 tablespoons finely chopped flat-leaf (Italian) parsley

Preheat the oven to 200°C (400°F/Gas 6). Bake the pistachio nuts on a lined baking tray for 5 minutes, or until golden brown. Cool, then finely chop.

Beat the cream cheese in a bowl until smooth. Fold in the dried apricot, spring onion and sun-dried tomato, and some freshly ground black pepper, to taste.

Sprinkle the combined pistachio nuts and parsley over a sheet of baking paper, shaping into a 20 x 6 cm (8 x 2½ inch) rectangle. Form the mixture into a 20 cm (8 inch) log and roll in the nut mixture. Wrap the log in plastic and refrigerate for 2–3 hours, or until firm. Serve with plain savoury biscuits.

Tomato and basil croustades

SERVES 4 PREPARATION TIME 30 minutes
COOKING TIME 20 minutes

- 1 day-old unsliced white bread loaf
- 3 tablespoons olive oil
- 2 garlic cloves, crushed
- 3 tomatoes, diced
- 250 g (9 oz) bocconcini (fresh baby mozzarella cheese), cut into small chunks
- 1 tablespoon tiny capers, rinsed and dried
- 1 tablespoon extra virgin olive oil
- 2 teaspoons balsamic vinegar
- 4 tablespoons shredded basil

Preheat the oven to 180°C (350°F/Gas 4). Remove the crusts from the bread and cut the loaf into four even pieces. Using a small serrated knife, cut a square from the centre of each cube of bread, leaving a border of about 1.5 cm (5/8 inch) on each side. You should be left with four 'boxes'. Combine the olive oil and garlic and brush all over the croustades. Place them on a baking tray and bake for about 20 minutes, or until golden and crisp. Check them occasionally to make sure they don't burn.

Meanwhile, combine the tomato and bocconcini with the tiny capers in a bowl.

In a bowl, stir together the extra virgin olive oil and balsamic vinegar, then gently toss with the tomato mixture. Season, to taste, with salt and freshly ground black pepper, then stir in the basil. Spoon into the croustades, allowing any excess to tumble over the sides.

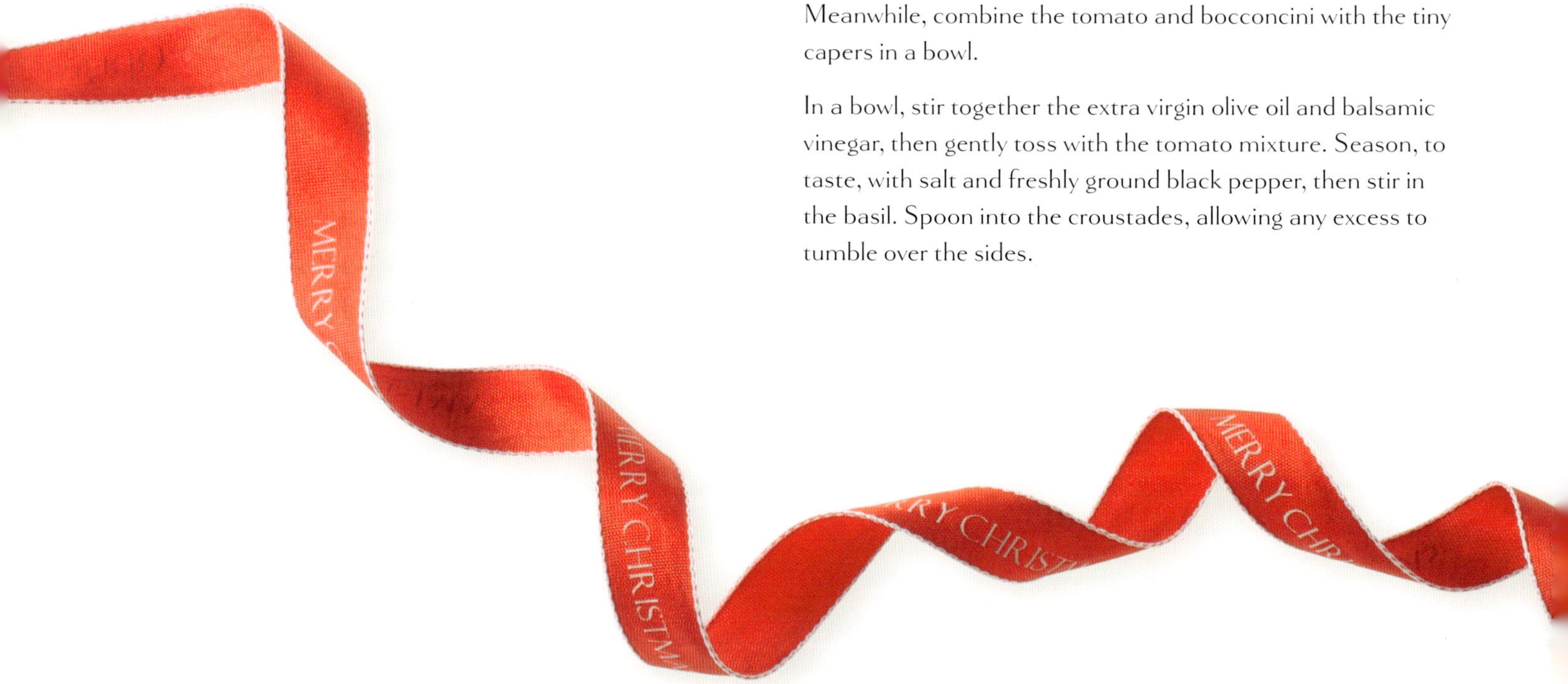

Herbed crêpe rolls

MAKES 24 PREPARATION TIME 20 minutes plus 30 minutes refrigeration COOKING TIME 25 minutes

- 2 eggs
- 85 g (3 oz/⅔ cup) plain (all-purpose) flour
- 200 ml (7 fl oz) milk
- ½ teaspoon baking powder
- 30 g (1 oz) butter, melted
- 20 g (¾ oz) butter, extra
- 3 tablespoons roughly chopped dill
- 2 tablespoons sliced spring onions (scallions)
- 100 g (3½ oz) shaved leg ham
- 130 g (4½ oz/1 cup) grated Jarlsberg cheese

Beat the eggs in a bowl, add the flour and milk a little at a time and beat to form a smooth batter. Add the baking powder and the melted butter, beat to combine, then refrigerate for 30 minutes. Just before using, remove the batter from the refrigerator and beat again to combine.

Heat 1 teaspoon of the extra butter in a non-stick frying pan over medium heat. When the butter begins to sizzle, pour in a quarter of the batter and swirl around the base of the pan to make a crêpe with a diameter of about 20 cm (8 inches). Sprinkle a quarter of the dill and spring onion over the crepe and cook for 2–3 minutes, or until bubbles appear on the surface. Carefully turn the crêpe over and cook for 1 minute before turning over once more. Remove and repeat with the remaining butter, batter, dill and spring onion to make four crêpes in total.

Fill the crêpes with the ham and grated cheese and roll up to form a log. Return to the pan and cook over low heat for 4–5 minutes, turning every minute or so, to melt the cheese inside. Remove, cool slightly and slice diagonally to serve.

Pesto palmiers

MAKES 60   PREPARATION TIME 20 minutes plus 30 minutes freezing   COOKING TIME 20 minutes per batch

- 1 large handful basil
- 1 garlic clove, crushed
- 3 tablespoons grated parmesan cheese
- 1 tablespoon pine nuts, toasted
- 2 tablespoons olive oil
- 4 sheets ready-rolled puff pastry, thawed

Preheat the oven to 220°C (425°F/Gas 7). Roughly chop the basil in a food processor with the garlic, parmesan and pine nuts. With the motor running, gradually add the oil in a thin stream and process until smooth.

Spread each pastry sheet with a quarter of the basil mixture. Roll up one side until you reach the middle, then repeat with the other side. Place on a tray. Repeat with the remaining pastry and basil mixture. Freeze for 30 minutes.

Slice each roll into 1.5 cm (5/8 inch) slices. Curl each slice into a semi-circle and place on a lightly greased baking tray. Allow room for the palmiers to expand during cooking. Bake them in batches for 15–20 minutes, or until golden brown.

NOTE: Other variations include spreading with a prepared tapenade paste made with olives, capers, anchovies, oil and garlic, or with tahini. Another simple version is to sprinkle just the grated parmesan between the pastry layers.

Mini eggs florentine

SERVES 24 PREPARATION TIME 20 minutes
COOKING TIME 25 minutes

8 slices white bread
1–2 tablespoons olive oil
12 quail eggs
2 teaspoons lemon juice
85 g (3 oz) butter, melted, cooled
2 teaspoons finely chopped basil
20 g (¾ oz) butter, extra
50 g (1¾ oz) baby English spinach leaves

Preheat the oven to 180°C (350°F/Gas 4). Cut 24 rounds from the bread with a 4 cm (1½ inch) cutter. Brush both sides of the rounds with the olive oil and bake for 10–15 minutes, or until golden brown.

Add the quail eggs to a small saucepan of cold water. Bring to the boil, stirring gently (to centre the yolk), then reduce the heat and simmer for 4 minutes. Drain, then soak in cold water until cool. Peel, then cut in half, remove the yolks and reserve the whites.

Process the quail egg yolks and lemon juice together in a food processor for 10 seconds. With the motor running, add the cooled melted butter in a thin stream. Add the chopped basil and process until combined.

Melt the extra butter in a saucepan, add the spinach leaves and toss until just wilted. Place a little on each bread round, top each with half a quail egg white and fill the cavity with the basil mixture.

Cranberry and apple martini

SERVES 6

3 tablespoons dry vermouth
crushed ice
270 ml (9½ fl oz) cloudy apple juice
185 ml (6 fl oz/¾ cup) gin
1½ tablespoons apple schnapps
90 ml (3 fl oz) cranberry juice
6 apple slices, such as royal gala, to serve

For the best result, mix one cocktail at a time. Pour 2 teaspoons of vermouth into a chilled martini glass and swirl to coat the sides. Discard the remaining liquid.

Half fill a cocktail shaker with the crushed ice, add 45 ml (1½ fl oz) of apple juice, 2½ tablespoons of gin, 1 teaspoon of apple schnapps and 3 teaspoons of cranberry juice. Stir and strain into the glass and garnish with a slice of apple. Repeat to make six martinis.

Blood orange Champagne cocktail

SERVES 4

125 ml (4 fl oz/½ cup) Campari
125 ml (4 fl oz/½ cup) blood orange juice
Champagne or sparkling white wine

Divide the Campari and orange juice among four cocktail glasses. Top with Champagne or sparkling wine and serve.

Eggnog

SERVES 6–8

4 eggs, separated
90 g (3¼ oz/⅓ cup) caster (superfine) sugar
315 ml (10¾ fl oz/1¼ cups) hot milk
125 ml (4 fl oz/½ cup) bourbon
125 ml (4 fl oz/½ cup) cream
grated nutmeg, for sprinkling

Beat the egg yolks and caster sugar in a heatproof bowl until light and fluffy. Add the hot milk and stir to combine.

Bring a saucepan of water to the boil, then reduce the heat until simmering. Place the bowl over the simmering water and stir with a wooden spoon for about 5–10 minutes, or until the mixture thickens and lightly coats the back of the spoon. Remove from the heat and allow to cool.

Stir in the bourbon. Beat the cream and the four egg whites in separate bowls until soft peaks form. Fold the cream, then the egg whites into the bourbon in two batches. Pour into glasses and sprinkle with grated nutmeg.

Brandy Alexander punch

SERVES 16

750 ml (26 fl oz/3 cups) brandy
375 ml (13 fl oz/1½ cups) crème de cacao (coffee liqueur)
1.75 litres (60 fl oz/7 cups) cream
ice cubes, to serve
grated nutmeg, for sprinkling
strawberries, to garnish

Pour the brandy, crème de cacao and cream into a large bowl. Whisk to just combine. Add ice cubes to a 3.5 litre (118 fl oz/14 cup) punch bowl and pour in the brandy mixture. Sprinkle with grated nutmeg, then serve in cocktail glasses garnished with strawberry halves.

Oysters with bloody mary sauce

MAKES 24 PREPARATION TIME 20 minutes
COOKING TIME nil

- 24 oysters on the half shell
- 3 tablespoons tomato juice
- 2 teaspoons vodka
- 1 teaspoon lemon juice
- ½ teaspoon worcestershire sauce
- 1–2 drops of Tabasco sauce
- 1 celery stick
- 1–2 teaspoons snipped chives

Remove the oysters from their shells and set aside. Wash the shells in hot water and pat dry. Combine the tomato juice, vodka, lemon juice, worcestershire sauce and Tabasco sauce in a small bowl.

Cut 1 celery stick into very thin julienne strips and place in the bases of the oyster shells. Top with an oyster and drizzle with the tomato mixture. Sprinkle with the snipped chives.

Tomato, chilli and coriander oysters

MAKES 24 PREPARATION TIME 25 minutes
COOKING TIME nil

- 24 oysters on the half shell
- 2 vine-ripened tomatoes, seeded and finely diced
- 2 French shallots, finely chopped
- 2 small red chillies, seeded and sliced
- 3 tablespoons chopped coriander (cilantro) leaves
- 1 tablespoon lime juice
- lime wedges, to serve

Remove the oysters from their shells and set aside. Wash the shells in hot water and pat dry. Replace the oysters and cover with a damp cloth in the refrigerator.

Put the tomato, shallots, chilli and coriander in a bowl and mix together well. Stir in the lime juice, then season, to taste, with salt and pepper. Put a teaspoon of salsa on each oyster. Serve with lime wedges for extra juice.

Champagne oysters

MAKES 24 PREPARATION TIME 10 minutes
COOKING TIME 30 minutes

1 French shallot, finely chopped
150 ml (10½ fl oz) Champagne or sparkling white wine
150 g (5½ oz) unsalted butter, cut into cubes
2 tablespoons crème fraîche
2 egg yolks
500 g (1 lb 2 oz) rock salt
24 oysters on the half shell

Put the shallot and 125 ml (4 fl oz/½ cup) of the Champagne in a small saucepan over medium heat. Simmer until reduced to 1 tablespoon. Strain into a heatproof bowl, discarding the shallot. Place the bowl over a saucepan of gently simmering water and whisk in the butter, one piece at a time, until thick and creamy. Remove from the heat. Stir in the crème fraîche.

Whisk the egg yolks and remaining Champagne in a separate heatproof bowl over a saucepan of gently simmering water until the mixture forms ribbons when drizzled. Remove from the heat and fold into the butter mixture. Lightly season.

Spread the rock salt on a baking tray and arrange the oysters on top. Spoon a teaspoon of the Champagne mixture onto each oyster and cook under a moderately hot grill (broiler) for 1–2 minutes, or until golden brown.

Oysters with prosciutto and balsamic vinegar

MAKES 24 PREPARATION TIME 15 minutes
COOKING TIME 1 minute

24 oysters on the half shell
2–3 tablespoons balsamic vinegar
6 slices prosciutto, each chopped into 4 thin strips

Remove the oysters from their shells and set aside. Wash the shells in hot water and pat dry. Replace the oysters and put them on a baking tray. Drizzle the balsamic vinegar over the oysters and arrange a coil of prosciutto on top. Season with cracked black pepper.

Cook under a hot grill (broiler) for about 1 minute, or until the prosciutto is starting to crisp.

Plum sauce

MAKES 1 litre (35 fl oz/4 cups) PREPARATION TIME 20 minutes COOKING TIME 1 hour

1 large green apple, peeled and chopped
16 blood plums (about 1.1 kg/2 lb 8 oz), halved, seeds intact
460 g (1 lb/2 cups) firmly packed soft brown sugar
375 ml (13 fl oz/1½ cups) white wine vinegar
3 tablespoons soy sauce
1 onion, shredded
2 tablespoons finely chopped fresh ginger
2 red chillies, seeded and finely chopped
2 garlic cloves, crushed

Put the apple in a large saucepan with 125 ml (4 fl oz/½ cup) water. Cover and simmer for 10 minutes, or until soft. Add the plums, sugar, vinegar, soy sauce, onion, ginger, chilli and garlic to the pan. Bring to the boil, then cook, uncovered, over low–medium heat for 45 minutes, stirring often.

Using a wooden spoon, press the sauce through a coarse strainer set over a large bowl. Discard the plum seeds. Return the sauce to the cleaned pan and return to the heat. Cook rapidly, stirring, until slightly thickened—it will thicken even more on cooling.

Immediately pour the sauce into clean, warm jars and seal. Turn the jars upside down for 2 minutes, then invert and let cool. Label and date. Leave for 1 month before opening to allow the flavours to develop. Store in a cool, dark place for up to 12 months. Refrigerate after opening for up to 6 weeks.

Blue cheese and port pâté

SERVES 8 PREPARATION TIME 10 minutes plus 3–4 hours refrigeration COOKING TIME nil

350 g (12 oz) cream cheese, at room temperature
60 g (2¼ oz) unsalted butter, softened
80 ml (2½ fl oz/⅓ cup) port
300 g (10½ oz) blue cheese, at room temperature, mashed
1 tablespoon chopped chives
50 g (1¾ oz/½ cup) walnut halves

Beat the cream cheese and butter in a small bowl with electric beaters until smooth, then stir in the port. Add the blue cheese and the chopped chives and stir until just combined. Season, to taste. Spoon into a serving dish and smooth the surface. Cover with plastic wrap and refrigerate for 3–4 hours, until the pâté is firm.

Arrange the walnut halves over the top of the pâté and press in lightly. Serve at room temperature. Delicious with crusty bread, crackers, celery sticks or wedges of firm fruit such as apple and pear.

Mini frittatas

SERVES 12 PREPARATION TIME 30 minutes
COOKING TIME 45 minutes

1 kg (2 lb 4 oz) orange sweet potato, cut into small cubes
1 tablespoon oil
30 g (1 oz) butter
4 leeks, white part only, finely sliced
2 garlic cloves, crushed
250 g (9 oz) feta cheese, crumbled
8 eggs
125 ml (4 fl oz/½ cup) cream

Preheat the oven to 180°C (350°F/Gas 4). Grease two trays of six 250 ml (9 fl oz/1 cup) muffin holes. Cut small rounds of baking paper and place one in the base of each hole.

Boil or steam the sweet potato until tender. Drain well and set aside.

Meanwhile, heat the oil and butter in a frying pan over low heat and cook the leek for 10 minutes, stirring occasionally, or until very soft and lightly golden. Add the garlic and cook for a further minute. Allow to cool, then stir in the feta and sweet potato. Divide the mixture among the muffin holes.

Whisk the eggs and cream together and season with salt and cracked black pepper. Pour the egg mixture into each hole until three-quarters filled. Bake for 25–30 minutes, or until golden and set. Leave in the tins for 5 minutes, then ease the frittatas out with a knife. Delicious served warm or at room temperature.

Refreshing juices

A colourful addition to the drinks menu, these fruity juices will be much appreciated by those needing a lift but not wishing to indulge in alcohol.

FRUIT SPARKLE

Pour 500 ml (17 fl oz/2 cups) chilled apricot nectar, 500 ml (17 fl oz/2 cups) chilled soda water, 250 ml (9 fl oz/1 cup) chilled apple juice and 250 ml (9 fl oz/1 cup) chilled orange juice into a large bowl and stir well. Stir in about 8 ice cubes, then pour into tall glasses and serve. Serves 4–6.

PASSIONFRUIT LIME CRUSH

Combine 125 g (4½ oz/½ cup) passionfruit pulp (you will need about 6 passionfruit), 185 ml (6 fl oz/¾ cup) lime juice cordial and 750 ml (26 fl oz/3 cups) ginger ale in a large bowl and mix together well. Pour into large glasses that have been half filled with crushed ice. Serve immediately. Serves 4.

RUBY GRAPEFRUIT AND LEMON SORBET FIZZ

Pour 500 ml (17 fl oz/2 cups) chilled ruby grapefruit juice and 250 ml (9 fl oz/1 cup) chilled soda water into a bowl. Stir in 1 tablespoon caster (superfine) sugar, then pour into chilled glasses. Top with a scoop of lemon sorbet. Mix the sorbet in or serve with a parfait spoon. Serves 4.

BLUEBERRY CRUSH

Blend 150 g (5 oz/1 cup) blueberries and 1 tablespoon caster (superfine) sugar in a blender until smooth. Mix with 750 ml (26 fl oz/3 cups) apple and blackcurrant juice and 500 ml (17 fl oz/2 cups) soda water. Serve immediately with ice in chilled glasses. If you have a good blender, you may wish to add the ice cubes when blending the blueberries, to make a slushy. Serves 4–6.

HAWAIIAN SMOOTHIE

Put 500 ml (17 fl oz/2 cups) chilled apple juice in a blender with 200 g (7 oz) peeled and seeded papaya or pawpaw, 400 g (14 oz) peeled and seeded watermelon and 20 ice cubes. Blend until smooth. Serves 4.

VIRGIN MARY

Stir 750 ml (26 fl oz/3 cups) tomato juice in a large bowl with 1 tablespoon worcestershire sauce, 2 tablespoons lemon juice, 1/4 teaspoon ground nutmeg and a few drops of Tabasco sauce until well mixed. Place 12 ice cubes in a blender and blend for 30 seconds, or until the ice is crushed. Spoon the ice into the tomato juice mixture, then carefully pour into tall glasses. Add a celery stick to each glass and decorate with very thin lemon slices. Season with salt and freshly ground black pepper, to taste, before serving. Serves 4.

MINT JULEP

Roughly chop 2 large handfuls mint leaves, place in a bowl and bruise with a wooden spoon. Transfer the mint to a heatproof bowl and add 2 tablespoons sugar, 1 tablespoon lemon juice, 500 ml (17 fl oz/2 cups) pineapple juice and 250 ml (9 fl oz/ 1 cup) boiling water. Mix, cover with plastic wrap and set aside for 30 minutes. Strain, then cover and refrigerate until well chilled. Mix in 500 ml (17 fl oz/2 cups) chilled ginger ale. Put ice cubes in glasses and pour in the drink. Garnish each glass with a few fresh mint leaves. Serves 4–6.

Starters

Stilton soup

SERVES 4–6 PREPARATION TIME 20 minutes
COOKING TIME 30 minutes

THYME PITTA CROUTONS
2 large Lebanese breads
1½ tablespoons thyme leaves
50 g (1¾ oz/½ cup) grated parmesan cheese

30 g (1 oz) butter
2 leeks, white part only, chopped
1 kg (2 lb 4 oz) potatoes, chopped
1.25 litres (44 fl oz/5 cups) chicken stock
125 ml (4 fl oz/½ cup) cream
100 g (3½ oz) Stilton cheese
thyme sprigs, to garnish

To make the croutons, preheat the oven to 180°C (350°F/Gas 4). Split each Lebanese bread into two, then cut each half into 8 wedges. Put the wedges on baking trays, sprinkle with the combined thyme and parmesan and bake in batches for 5–8 minutes each batch, or until golden and crisp.

Melt the butter in a large saucepan, add the leek and cook until softened. Add the potato and stock and bring to the boil. Simmer, covered, for 15 minutes, or until the potato is tender (pierce with the point of a knife—if the potato comes away easily, it is cooked).

Transfer the potato mixture, in batches if necessary, to a blender or food processor and blend until smooth. Return to the saucepan and add the cream and cheese. Stir over low heat until the cheese has melted, being careful not to let the mixture boil. Ladle into individual dishes and garnish with thyme sprigs. Serve with the thyme pitta croutons.

NOTE: The croutons can be made up to a week ahead and stored in an airtight container. If they soften, spread them on a baking tray and bake in a 160°C (315°F/Gas 2–3) oven for 2–3 minutes.

Jerusalem artichoke and chestnut soup

SERVES 8 PREPARATION TIME 20 minutes
COOKING TIME 1 hour 20 minutes

350 g (12 oz) fresh chestnuts
1.25 kg (2 lb 12 oz) jerusalem artichokes, peeled and chopped
2 tablespoons olive oil
1 onion, finely chopped
2 garlic cloves, crushed
1 boiling potato, peeled and chopped
2 litres (70 fl oz/8 cups) chicken stock
50 g ($1\frac{3}{4}$ oz) butter, softened
90 ml (3 fl oz) cream

Preheat the oven to 180°C (350°F/Gas 4). Score a small cross on the base of each chestnut and place on a baking tray. Bake for 20–25 minutes, until the skins start to split. Wrap the chestnuts in a tea towel (dish towel) and leave for 5 minutes, then peel, one at a time, removing the outer and inner skin. Set aside to cool, then finely chop.

Place the jerusalem artichokes on a baking tray, drizzle with 1 tablespoon of the olive oil, season with sea salt and bake for 30 minutes, or until lightly coloured.

Heat the remaining olive oil in a saucepan over low heat and cook the onion and garlic for 5 minutes, or until soft. Add the artichoke, potato and stock and simmer for 20 minutes, or until the potato and artichoke are soft. Add the butter and cream, stir to combine and simmer gently for 1 minute. Allow to cool slightly and blend, in batches, until smooth.

Return the soup to the cleaned saucepan and gently reheat over low heat. Season with sea salt and freshly ground black pepper and serve sprinkled with the toasted chestnuts.

Spiced pumpkin soup with ginger cream

- SERVES 4–6
- PREPARATION TIME 20 minutes
- COOKING TIME 30 minutes

1 teaspoon cumin seeds
1 tablespoon olive oil
1 onion, finely chopped
1 garlic clove, crushed
1 teaspoon grated fresh ginger
1 teaspoon ground cumin
1 teaspoon ground coriander
¼ teaspoon dried chilli flakes
750 g (1 lb 10 oz) pumpkin (winter squash), chopped
1 litre (35 fl oz/4 cups) vegetable stock
100 g (3½ oz) piece speck, sliced into thin strips
1 tablespoon finely chopped coriander (cilantro) leaves

GINGER CREAM

90 g (3¼ oz/⅓ cup) sour cream
80 ml (2½ fl oz/⅓ cup) cream
1 teaspoon grated fresh ginger
1 teaspoon lemon juice
1 tablespoon finely chopped coriander (cilantro) leaves

Place the cumin seeds in a small frying pan and cook over medium heat until fragrant. Crush using a mortar and pestle until finely ground.

Heat the oil in a large saucepan, add the onion and cook over medium heat for 2 minutes, or until just soft. Add the garlic, ginger, cumin, ground coriander and chilli flakes and cook, stirring constantly, until fragrant. Add the pumpkin and stock and bring to the boil. Reduce the heat to low and simmer, uncovered, for 20 minutes, or until the pumpkin is tender.

Meanwhile, fry the speck in a small frying pan over high heat until golden brown and crisp.

To make the ginger cream, combine the sour cream, cream, ginger and lemon juice in a small bowl and beat until slightly thickened. Fold in the coriander.

Blend or process the soup until smooth. Return the soup to the cleaned saucepan and reheat gently over low heat. Ladle into serving bowls and top with a dollop of ginger cream, a sprinkle of coriander and a few pieces of speck.

Gravlax

SERVES 20 PREPARATION TIME 20 minutes plus 24 hours refrigeration COOKING TIME nil

- 3 tablespoons sugar
- 2 tablespoons coarse sea salt
- 1 teaspoon crushed black peppercorns
- 2.5 kg (5 lb 8 oz) salmon, filleted and boned but with the skin left on (ask your fishmonger to do this)
- 1 tablespoon vodka or brandy
- 4 tablespoons very finely chopped dill

MUSTARD SAUCE

- 1½ tablespoons cider vinegar
- 1 teaspoon caster (superfine) sugar
- 125 ml (4 fl oz/½ cup) olive oil
- 2 teaspoons chopped dill
- 2 tablespoons dijon mustard

Combine the sugar, sea salt and peppercorns in a small dish. Remove any bones from the salmon fillets with tweezers. Pat dry with paper towels and lay one fillet, skin side down, in a shallow tray or baking dish. Sprinkle with half of the vodka or brandy, rub half the sugar mixture into the flesh, then sprinkle with half the dill. Sprinkle the remaining vodka or brandy over the second salmon fillet and rub the remaining sugar mixture into the flesh. Lay it flesh side down on top of the dill-coated salmon. Cover with plastic wrap, place a heavy board on top and weigh it down with heavy food cans or a brick covered with foil. Refrigerate for 24 hours, turning the salmon over after 12 hours.

To make the mustard sauce, whisk together the ingredients, then cover until needed.

When the salmon is ready, take off the weights and remove the plastic wrap. Lift off the top fillet and lay both fillets on a wooden board. Brush off the dill and any seasoning mixture with a stiff pastry brush. Sprinkle with the remaining fresh dill and press it onto the salmon flesh, shaking off any excess.

Serve the salmon whole on the serving board and thinly slice, as required, on an angle towards the tail. Serve with the mustard sauce.

NOTES: Gravlax can be refrigerated, covered, for up to a week. It can also be frozen. Use a very sharp knife with a long flexible blade to slice the salmon. A filleting knife is ideal.

Scallops en brochette

SERVES 6 PREPARATION TIME 15 minutes
COOKING TIME 10 minutes

36 scallops
8–10 slices prosciutto
8–10 spring onions (scallions)
60 g (2¼ oz) butter, melted
1 garlic clove, crushed
2 tablespoons lime juice
lime slices or wedges, for serving

If you are using wooden skewers, soak them in cold water for 30 minutes to prevent them burning during cooking.

Slice or pull off any vein, membrane or hard white muscle from the scallops, leaving the roe attached. Cut each slice of prosciutto into three pieces and gently wrap a piece of prosciutto around each scallop. Cut the spring onions into short lengths. Thread them onto skewers, alternating three scallops and three pieces of spring onion on each skewer.

Cook the scallops on a preheated grill (broiler) or barbecue for 3–5 minutes each side, or until the prosciutto is lightly browned and the scallops are just cooked through. Brush occasionally with the combined melted butter, garlic and lime juice. Serve the scallops with any of the remaining warm butter mixture and lime slices.

SANTA

The origin of the story of Saint Nicholas goes back as far as a legend in the fourth century that personifies Santa Claus as a holy man named Nicholas. He entered the priesthood as a teenager and later became a Bishop. It is claimed he performed many miracles. He was made a saint after his death. The anniversary of his death, December 6, became a feast day on the church calendar. He became the patron saint of many people and it was claimed he roamed the earth on his feast day every year leaving sweets and trinkets in children's shoes. Thomas Nast, a cartoonist, depicted the saint in a red suit for Harper's Weekly in 1863. This concept of Santa has remained unchanged.

The poem 'A Visit from St. Nicholas' is largely responsible for many of the traditions surrounding Santa Claus that are celebrated today. Also known as 'The Night Before Christmas', the poem was first published anonymously in 1823. It describes Santa Claus arriving in a sleigh drawn by flying reindeer, and the 'chubby and plump ... right jolly old elf' descending down the chimney to deliver gifts to sleeping children.

Raised pork pie

SERVES 6–8
PREPARATION TIME 20 minutes plus chilling and overnight setting
COOKING TIME 1 hour 5 minutes

- 1.2 kg (2 lb 10 oz) minced (ground) pork
- 90 g (3¼ oz/⅔ cup) chopped pistachio nuts
- 2 green apples, peeled and finely chopped
- 6 sage leaves, finely chopped
- 500 g (1 lb 2 oz/4 cups) plain (all-purpose) flour
- 150 g (5½ oz) butter
- 2 eggs, lightly beaten
- 1 egg yolk, to glaze
- 200 ml (7 fl oz) vegetable stock
- 200 ml (7 fl oz) unsweetened apple juice
- 2 teaspoons gelatine

Mix together the pork, pistachio nuts, apple and sage, and season. Fry a piece of the mixture to taste and adjust the seasoning. Cover and refrigerate.

Wrap a piece of plastic wrap around a straight-sided 6 cm (2½ inch) high, 20 cm (8 inch) tin, then turn the tin over and grease the outside base and side.

Put the flour and 1 teaspoon salt in a bowl and make a well in the centre. Put the butter in a pan with 210 ml (7½ fl oz) water, bring to the boil and add to the flour with the egg. Mix with a wooden spoon until combined, then turn out onto a work surface and bring together to form a smooth dough. Wrap in plastic wrap and refrigerate for 10 minutes.

Cut off a third of the pastry and wrap in plastic wrap—do not refrigerate. Roll the remainder into a circle large enough to just cover the outside of the tin. Lift onto a rolling pin and place over the tin, working fast before the pastry sets. Refrigerate until the pastry hardens (about 3 hours).

Preheat the oven to 200°C (400°F/Gas 6). Line a baking tray with baking paper. Carefully pull the tin out from inside the pastry case and remove the plastic wrap. Attach a paper collar made of two layers of greased baking paper around the outside of the pastry so it fits snugly, and secure with a paperclip at the top and bottom. Put the pastry case on the baking tray. Fill the pie with the pork mixture, then roll out the remaining pastry to form a lid. Attach it to the base with some water, pressing or crimping around the edge. Cut a small hole in the top of the pie.

Bake the pie for 40 minutes and check the pastry top. If it is still pale, bake for a further 10 minutes, then remove the paper. Brush with the egg yolk mixed with 1 tablespoon water and bake for another 15 minutes, or until the sides are brown. Cool completely.

Bring the stock and half the apple juice to the boil. Sprinkle the gelatine over the surface of the remaining apple juice in a bowl and leave to go spongy, then pour into the stock and mix until the gelatine dissolves. Place a small funnel (a piping or icing nozzle works well) in the hole of the pie and pour in a little of the gelatine, leave to settle, then pour in some more until the pie is full. Fill the pie completely so there are no gaps when the gelatine sets. Leave in the refrigerator overnight.

NOTE: If wrapped tightly with plastic wrap, pork pies will last for 4–5 days in the refrigerator.

Game terrine

SERVES 10 PREPARATION TIME 30 minutes plus overnight refrigeration COOKING TIME 55 minutes

310 g (11 oz) duck, squab or guinea fowl meat, coarsely minced (ground)
200 g (7 oz) pork shoulder, coarsely minced (ground)
230 g (8¼ oz) pork back fat, coarsely minced (ground)
1 tablespoon Cognac
1 tablespoon Madeira
2 tablespoons chicken stock
1 egg yolk
½ teaspoon finely grated orange zest
2 tablespoons pistachio nuts
½ teaspoon chopped thyme
1 garlic clove, crushed
2 teaspoons salt
½ teaspoon freshly ground black pepper
pinch of cloves
pinch of freshly grated nutmeg
1 juniper berry, crushed
pinch of ground ginger
10 slices prosciutto
2 bay leaves
toasted brioche, to serve

Preheat the oven to 120°C (235°F/Gas ½). Line a 24 x 7.5 cm (9½ x 3 inch) terrine tin with two layers of plastic wrap, making sure there is plenty of overhang.

Combine the duck, squab or guinea fowl, pork shoulder and pork fat in a large mixing bowl. Add the Cognac, Madeira, stock, egg yolk, orange zest, pistachio nuts, thyme, garlic, salt, pepper and spices and mix well.

Line the base and sides of the terrine tin with the prosciutto, overlapping the slices slightly and allowing them to overhang the two long edges of the tin. Spoon in the duck mixture and press firmly into the sides and corners. Smooth the surface and fold the overhanging prosciutto over the filling. Lay the bay leaves on top. Cover with the overhanging plastic wrap.

Place the terrine in a roasting tin. Fill the roasting tin with boiling water to come halfway up the sides of the terrine tin. Bake for 55 minutes, or until the juices run clear when a skewer is inserted in the centre of the terrine. Remove the terrine from the roasting tin and refrigerate overnight. Cut into slices and serve with the brioche.

Camembert and potato terrine

SERVES 8–10 PREPARATION TIME 1 hour plus overnight refrigeration COOKING TIME 55 minutes

6 new potatoes, unpeeled
3 green apples
125 g (4½ oz) butter
3 tablespoons olive oil
200 g (7 oz) camembert, chilled and very thinly sliced
2 tablespoons chopped flat-leaf (Italian) parsley

Parboil the potatoes in lightly salted water for 15 minutes. Drain and cool, then peel and cut into 1 cm (½ inch) slices.

Core the apples and slice into 5 mm (¼ inch) thick rounds.

Heat half the butter and half the oil in a large frying pan and cook the potato until just golden. Drain on crumpled paper towels. Heat the remaining butter and oil in the pan. Lightly fry the sliced apple until golden, then remove and drain on crumpled paper towels.

Preheat the oven to 180°C (350°F/Gas 4). Line a 25 x 11 cm (10 x 4½ inch) terrine tin with baking paper. Arrange a layer of potato in the base of the terrine. Add a layer of apple, then camembert. Sprinkle with parsley and season with salt and pepper, to taste. Build up the layers, finishing with potato.

Brush a piece of foil with oil and cover the terrine, sealing it well. Place the terrine in a roasting tin and fill the roasting tin with boiling water to come halfway up the sides of the terrine tin. Bake for 20 minutes, then remove from the roasting tin. Cover with foil, then put a piece of heavy cardboard, cut to fit, on top of the terrine. Put weights or food cans on top of the cardboard to compress the terrine. Refrigerate overnight. Turn out and slice, to serve.

LANTERN CANDLE HOLDER

The glow of flickering candlelight is increased and refracted by rows of seed beads in these glittering lanterns, which would make a stunning table decoration or Christmas gift. Don't be daunted by the number of beads used in the construction: the method is quite simple and surprisingly quick to complete.

MATERIALS

- For the small lantern: 864 round Indian glass beads, 4 mm (3/16 inch) diameter
- For the large lantern: 1560 round Indian glass beads, 4 mm (3/16 inch) diameter
- Artist's wire, gold 0.7 mm (21 gauge)

TOOLS

- Round-nose pliers
- Snipe-nose pliers
- Side cutters
- Safety glasses
- Ruler

1 Cut the artist's wire with the side cutters into six 70 cm (20 inch) lengths. Bend each length in half and set them aside.

2 Unwind the remaining artist's wire, keeping it coiled. Using the round-nose pliers, grasp the wire 2.5 cm (1 inch) from the end and bend it around the pliers. Hold the end of the wire with the snipe-nose pliers and wrap it 360 degrees around the length of the wire in a full circle to make a wrapped loop. Cut off the excess wire so that only a loop is left at the end of the wire.

3 Thread all of the beads onto the coiled wire, carefully moving them along to the end of the wire, while still keeping it coiled.

4 Thread the wires made in Step 1 onto the beaded coil, placing the first wire through the looped end of the beaded coil. Continue to thread wires 2 to 5 along the beaded coil, placing a bead in between each wire (see photograph). Secure the long wires around the coil by pulling them open in opposite directions.

5 Form the base of the lantern by continuing to wrap the beads around the initial loop, forming a flat disc. Secure each rotation of the beads with the long wires by passing them around either side of the coil. Expand the base by adding an extra bead in between the wires on each roation (see photograph) until there are eight beads in between each wire. Push the beads tightly together after completing each coil so that the lantern is even.

6 Construct the vertical walls of the lantern by continuing to coil and secure the beads, maintaining eight beads in each section. The first row of the wall should rest on top of the last row of the base. Continue to secure the coils until all the beads are used.

7 Once all the beads are secured, twist the remaining lengths of doubled wire for approximately 20 mm (3/4 inch), cut off any excess with side cutters and bend the wires so they sit inside the lantern. Push the lantern into a cylindrical shape.

STEP 2 Create a noose at the end of the wire, then thread all of the beads on.

STEP 4 Add the spokes of doubled wire to the beaded coil.

STEP 5 Construct the flat base of the lantern.

STEP 6 Create the vertical sides of the lantern.

Prawn and papaya salad

SERVES 4 PREPARATION TIME 25 minutes
COOKING TIME nil

750 g (1 lb 10 oz) large cooked prawns (shrimp)
1 large papaya
1 small red onion, finely sliced
2 celery sticks, finely sliced
2 tablespoons shredded mint leaves

DRESSING
125 ml (4 fl oz/½ cup) oil
3 tab lespoons lime juice
2 teaspoons finely grated fresh ginger
1 teaspoon caster (superfine) sugar

Peel the prawns, leaving the tails intact. Gently pull out the dark vein from each prawn back, starting at the head end. Place in a large bowl.

For the dressing, put all the ingredients in a small bowl and whisk to combine. Season, to taste, with salt and freshly ground black pepper.

Add the dressing to the prawns and toss gently to coat. Peel the papaya, remove the seeds and cut into bite-sized chunks. Add the papaya, onion, celery and mint to the prawns and toss. Serve the salad immediately or cover and refrigerate for up to 3 hours before serving.

Prawn cocktails

SERVES 4 PREPARATION TIME 20 minutes
COOKING TIME nil

3 tablespoons whole-egg mayonnaise
2 teaspoons tomato sauce (ketchup)
dash of Tabasco sauce
¼ teaspoon worcestershire sauce
2 teaspoons thick (double/heavy) cream
¼ teaspoon lemon juice
24 cooked large prawns (shrimp)
4 lettuce leaves, shredded
lemon wedges, for serving

Mix the mayonnaise, sauces, cream and juice together in a small bowl.

Peel the prawns, leaving the tails intact on eight of them. Gently pull out the dark vein from the back of each prawn, starting at the head end.

Divide the lettuce among four glasses. Arrange the prawns without the tails in the glasses and drizzle with the sauce. Hang two of the remaining prawns over the edge of each glass and serve with lemon wedges.

Pickled prawns

SERVES 4–6 PREPARATION TIME 20 minutes plus 48 hours refrigeration COOKING TIME nil

- 40 cooked large prawns (shrimp)
- 1 fennel bulb (600 g (1 lb 5 oz)
- 2 small red onions, thinly sliced
- 2 tablespoons thin strips of orange rind
- 2 tablespoons thin strips of lime rind
- 125 ml (4 fl oz/½ cup) lime juice
- 80 ml (2½ fl oz/⅓ cup) orange juice
- 250 ml (9 fl oz/1 cup) olive oil
- 125 ml (4 fl oz/½ cup) tarragon vinegar
- 2 red birds-eye chillies, finely sliced
- 1 teaspoon sugar

Peel the prawns, leaving the tails intact. Gently pull out the dark vein from each prawn back, starting at the head end. Thinly slice the fennel, reserving some of the green fronds. Place the prawns, fennel, onion and orange and lime rind in a non-metallic bowl and mix well.

Mix the remaining ingredients together, add 1 teaspoon salt and pour over the prawn mixture. Cover and refrigerate for 48 hours, stirring once or twice.

Garnish the prawns with the reserved fennel fronds and serve with fresh crusty bread and a mixed salad.

Festive prawn salad

SERVES 8 PREPARATION TIME 30 minutes COOKING TIME 10 minutes

ROUILLE

- 1 small red capsicum (pepper)
- 1 red chilli, seeded
- 1 slice white bread, crusts removed
- 2 garlic cloves, halved
- 1 egg yolk
- 1 tablespoon lime juice
- 3 tablespoons olive oil

- 2 kg (4 lb 8 oz) cooked prawns (shrimp), peeled and deveined
- 100 g (3½ oz) baby English spinach
- 100 g (3½ oz) baby rocket (arugula) leaves
- 2 tablespoons extra virgin olive oil
- 1 tablespoon lemon juice
- 3 avocados, sliced

For the rouille, cut the capsicum and chilli into flattish pieces. Cook, skin side up, under a hot grill (broiler) until the skin blackens. Cool in a plastic bag, then peel. Soak the bread in 3 tablespoons water, squeeze out the excess and blend with the capsicum, chilli, garlic, egg yolk and lime juice in a food processor. With the motor running, gradually add the oil.

Mix the prawns with half the rouille. Toss the spinach and rocket with the oil and lemon juice and top with the avocado and prawn mixture. Serve with extra rouille.

Salmon and fennel frittata

SERVES 8 PREPARATION TIME 35 minutes
COOKING TIME 1 hour 15 minutes

- 1½ tablespoons olive oil
- 1 onion, finely chopped
- 1 fennel bulb (about 280 g/ 10 oz), finely chopped
- 3 tablespoons white wine
- 60 g (2¼ oz) watercress sprigs
- 12 eggs
- 435 ml (15¼ fl oz/1¾ cups) cream
- 3 tablespoons chopped dill
- 50 g (1¾ oz/½ cup) grated parmesan cheese
- 300 g (10½ oz) smoked salmon, cut into strips

Preheat the oven to 180°C (350°F/Gas 4). Lightly grease a 22 cm (9 inch) springform tin and line the base and side with baking paper, making sure you have a tight seal all the way around the tin. Place the tin on a baking tray in case it leaks.

Heat the oil in a heavy-based saucepan and add the onion, fennel and a pinch of salt. Cook over low heat for 5 minutes, stirring occasionally. Add the wine and cook for another 5 minutes, or until the vegetables are tender. Remove from the heat and leave to cool.

Finely chop half the watercress and divide the remainder into small sprigs. Beat the eggs lightly in a bowl, then add the cream, dill, parmesan, chopped watercress, and onion and fennel mixture. Season, to taste, with salt and black pepper.

Pour half the egg mixture into the prepared tin, sprinkle with 200 g (6½ oz) smoked salmon and pour in the remaining egg mixture. Bake for 1 hour, or until the frittata is set in the centre and golden on the surface. Remove from the pan and peel off the baking paper from the side. Invert onto a plate and remove the paper from the base. Invert onto a serving dish and arrange the remaining salmon and watercress on top. Cut into wedges and serve warm.

Bruschetta with Mediterranean toppings

MAKES 12 PREPARATION TIME 20 minutes
COOKING TIME 15 minutes

CAPSICUM TOPPING
1 yellow capsicum (pepper)
1 red capsicum (pepper)
1 green capsicum (pepper)
1 tablespoon chopped flat-leaf (Italian) parsley

TOMATO BASIL TOPPING
2 ripe tomatoes
3 tablespoons shredded basil
1 tablespoon extra virgin olive oil

12 slices crusty Italian bread
2 garlic cloves, halved
80 ml (2½ fl oz/⅓ cup) extra virgin olive oil

To make the capsicum topping, cut all the capsicums into large, flattish pieces and cook, skin side up, under a hot grill (broiler) until the skin blackens and blisters. Place in a plastic bag until cool, then peel. Slice the flesh into strips.

To make the tomato and basil topping, finely chop the tomatoes and combine in a bowl with the basil and olive oil. Season with black pepper.

Toast the bread and, while still hot, rub with the cut side of a garlic clove. Drizzle olive oil over each slice and sprinkle with salt and plenty of freshly ground black pepper.

Arrange the capsicum on half the bread slices, then sprinkle with the parsley. Arrange the tomato and basil topping on the remaining bread slices. Serve immediately.

Pumpkin tarts

SERVES 6 PREPARATION TIME 20 minutes plus 30 minutes refrigeration COOKING TIME 35 minutes

250 g (9 oz/2 cups) plain (all-purpose) flour
125 g (4½ oz) butter, chilled and cubed
1.2 kg (2 lb 10 oz) pumpkin, cut into 6 cm (2½ inch) pieces
125 g (4½ oz/½ cup) sour cream or cream cheese
sweet chilli sauce, for serving

Sift the flour and a pinch of salt into a large bowl and rub in the chopped butter with your fingertips until the mixture resembles fine breadcrumbs. Make a well in the centre and add 80 ml (2½ fl oz/⅓ cup) of iced water. Mix with a flat-bladed knife, using a cutting action until the mixture comes together in beads. Gently gather the dough together and lift out onto a lightly floured work surface. Press into a ball and flatten into a disc, then wrap in plastic wrap and refrigerate for 30 minutes.

Preheat the oven to 200°C (400°F/Gas 6). Divide the pastry into six portions and roll each one out to fit into a 10 cm (4 inch) pie dish. Trim the edges and prick the bases all over. Place on a baking tray and bake for 15 minutes, or until lightly golden, pressing down any pastry that puffs up. Cool, then remove from the tins.

Meanwhile, steam the pumpkin for about 15 minutes, or until tender.

Place 1 tablespoon of sour cream or cream cheese in the middle of each pastry case and pile some of the pumpkin pieces on top. Season with salt and cracked black pepper and drizzle with sweet chilli sauce. Return to the oven for a couple of minutes to heat through. Serve immediately.

Chargrilled vegetable terrine

SERVES 8 PREPARATION TIME 30 minutes plus overnight refrigeration COOKING TIME nil

- 350 g (12 oz) ricotta
- 2 garlic cloves, crushed
- 8 slices chargrilled eggplant (aubergine), drained
- 10 slices chargrilled red capsicum (pepper), drained
- 8 slices chargrilled zucchini (courgette), drained
- 45 g (1½ oz) rocket (arugula) leaves
- 3 marinated artichokes, drained and sliced
- 85 g (3 oz) semi-dried (sun-blushed) tomatoes, drained and chopped
- 100 g (3½ oz) marinated mushrooms, drained and halved

Line a 23.5 x 13 x 6.5 cm (9 x 5 x 2½ inch) loaf tin with plastic wrap, leaving a generous amount hanging over the sides. Place the ricotta and garlic in a bowl and beat until smooth. Season well and set aside.

Line the base of the prepared tin with half the eggplant, cutting and fitting to cover the base. Top with a layer of half the capsicum, then all the zucchini slices. Spread with the ricotta mixture and press down firmly. Place the rocket on top of the ricotta mixture. Arrange the artichoke, semi-dried tomato and mushroom in three rows on top of the ricotta.

Top with another layer of capsicum and finish with the rest of the eggplant. Cover securely with the overlapping plastic wrap. Put a piece of cardboard on top of the terrine and weigh it down with small food cans. Refrigerate overnight.

Peel back the plastic wrap and invert the terrine onto a plate. Remove the plastic wrap and cut into thick slices.

NOTE: Chargrilled vegetables and marinated mushrooms and artichokes are available at delicatessens.

Pork and veal terrine

SERVES 6 PREPARATION TIME 20 minutes plus overnight refrigeration COOKING TIME 1 hour 20 minutes

8–10 thin bacon slices
1 tablespoon olive oil
1 onion, chopped
2 garlic cloves, crushed
1 kg (2 lb 4 oz) minced (ground) pork and veal
80 g (2¾ oz/1 cup) fresh breadcrumbs
1 egg, beaten
3 tablespoons brandy
3 teaspoons chopped thyme
3 tablespoons chopped parsley

Preheat the oven to 180°C (350°F/Gas 4). Lightly grease a 25 x 11 cm (10 x 4½ inch) terrine tin. Line the tin with the bacon so that it overlaps slightly and hangs over the sides.

Heat the olive oil in a frying pan, add the onion and garlic and cook for 2–3 minutes, or until the onion is soft. Cool, then mix with the pork and veal, breadcrumbs, egg, brandy, thyme and parsley in a large bowl. Season with some salt and pepper. Fry a small piece of the mixture to check the seasoning, and adjust if necessary.

Spoon the mixture into the bacon-lined terrine, pressing down firmly to avoid any air bubbles. Fold the bacon over the top of the terrine, cover with lightly greased foil and place in a roasting tin.

Fill the roasting tin with boiling water to come halfway up the sides of the terrine. Bake for 1–1¼ hours, or until the juices run clear when the terrine is pierced with a skewer. Remove the terrine from the roasting tin and pour off the excess juices.

Cover the terrine with foil, then put a piece of heavy cardboard, cut to fit, on top of the terrine. Put weights or heavy food cans on top of the cardboard to compress the terrine. Refrigerate overnight, then cut into slices to serve.

NOTE: The terrine can be made ahead of time. Cover and store in the refrigerator for up to 5 days.

Beetroot salad with goat's cheese

SERVES 6
PREPARATION TIME 20 minutes
COOKING TIME 1 hour 10 minutes

1½ tablespoons olive oil
4 beetroot (beets), scrubbed
125 ml (4 fl oz/½ cup) red wine
2 tablespoons red wine vinegar
2 tablespoons soft brown sugar
8 cloves
120 g (4¼ oz) goat's cheese
125 ml (4 fl oz/½ cup) cream, for whipping
thyme leaves, to serve
toasted brioche, to serve

Preheat the oven to 220°C (425°F/Gas 7).

Lightly rub 1 tablespoon of the oil into the beetroot. Wrap each beetroot in foil, place on a large baking tray and roast for 1 hour, or until tender when pierced with a skewer. Remove from the oven and allow to cool slightly. Peel the beetroot and thinly slice using a sharp knife or mandolin.

Combine the wine, vinegar, sugar and cloves in a saucepan over medium–high heat and bring to the boil. Reduce the heat to low and simmer for 5 minutes, or until slightly syrupy. Remove from the heat, add the beetroot and allow to cool.

Meanwhile, place the cheese and cream in a bowl and beat using electric beaters until pale and fluffy, about 3 minutes.

Drain the beetroot, reserving the liquid. Whisk 3 tablespoons of the reserved beetroot poaching liquid with the remaining oil.

Divide the beetroot among six serving plates, slightly overlapping the slices, and dot with the whipped goat's cheese. Drizzle on the dressing and scatter with the thyme leaves. Serve with the toasted brioche.

Mains

HOW TO CARVE

• Carving a roast can be tricky, so follow these instructions and even the most inexperienced carver will be able to serve a perfect Christmas roast in a quick and fuss-free manner. Turkey and ham are traditionally the most popular Christmas roasts—and the most daunting. They are rarely eaten at other times of the year and can easily confound the most confident of cooks when it comes to carving them.

• Before carving any roast, it is important to let the meat 'rest' for 15 minutes or so. Remove the roast from the oven and cover it with foil so the heat does not escape too quickly. The 'resting' allows the juices to settle and distribute evenly, moistening and tenderising the flesh.

Ham

1 After it has rested, place the ham on a cutting board with the bone to the left. Use a clean tea towel to hold the bone firmly while carving. Remember to keep your fingers away from the blade! Slice a piece from the underside of the leg so that it sits flat on the board. Remove this slice and set aside.

2 Slice into the meat about 10 cm (4 inches) from the knuckle. Make another cut at an angle to the first so that it forms a wedge, then remove. Continue cutting to the right, cutting several thin slices right down to the bone. The meat will still be attached to the bone so to release the pieces you must run the knife along the bone, under the meat. Use the flat of the knife to lift off the slices. Cut enough slices for serving, covering the slices with foil as you go if the ham is to be served warm.

Cut a slice from the underside of the ham to steady it while carving.

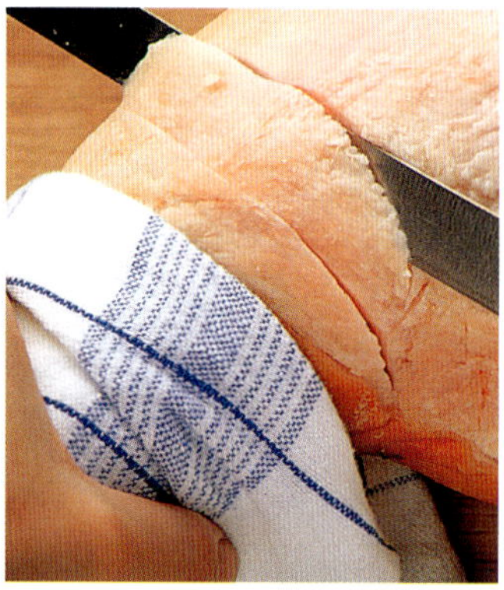

Remove a wedge of ham from the knuckle end before you carve.

Cut thin slices, working away from the knuckle.

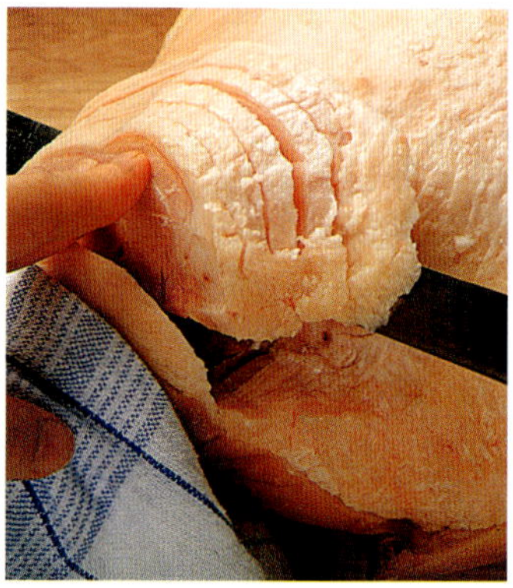

Cut the slices away from the bone and serve.

- Make sure your carving knife is sharp and try to slice rather than saw—the more you hack into the meat, tearing the flesh, the more juices are lost, making the meat dry. Electric knives can make life much easier. A carving fork is also important for holding the meat steady. Do not pierce the meat—try to use the back of the fork to get a good hold. When carving a bird, however, a sharp-pronged fork is needed to dig deep into the carcass (not the flesh) to keep it still.

- Always carve on a carving board, not a serving platter. China and metal surfaces can scratch easily and can be quite slippery, causing you to lose control of the knife. It is preferable to use a carving board with a rim to catch any excess juices—this not only stops the juices from spilling over onto the table but it also means they can be strained off and used in your gravy for an extra boost of flavour. It is also a good idea to place a damp cloth underneath your board to keep it steady while carving.

Turkey

1 After it has rested, place the turkey on a cutting board, breast side up and with the legs facing you.

2 Use a carving fork to steady the bird and cut downward into the skin and meat where the leg meets the breast. Bend the leg outwards with the carving knife until you can see the joint where the thighbone and the backbone connect. Keep cutting at a slight angle towards the joint, then cut down and through it until the leg section (the thigh and drumstick) can be easily removed. Depending on the size of the turkey, you can also cut through the leg at the joint to remove the thigh and have two separate pieces. Set the meat aside on a warm serving dish and keep covered with foil while you are carving the rest of the turkey. This will keep it warm and stop it from drying out.

3 On the same side of the bird, find where the wing meets the body and cut down, again until you meet the joint. You may need to pull the wing out with one hand while you are cutting with the other to loosen the wing from the bird. Set aside and cover to keep warm.

4 Continuing on the same side, begin to carve the breast. Start at the top of the breast where it attaches to the ridge of bone and carve downwards in even slices, at a slight angle, towards the cutting board. Add to the rest of the meat. Now repeat this process on the other side of the turkey. To remove the wishbone, snip the sinews on either side.

5 Remove the stuffing from the opening of the carcass with a spoon and, depending on the texture of the stuffing, serve it either in slices or in spoonfuls.

Remove the leg and thigh section from the body of the turkey.

With larger birds it is possible to separate the leg and thigh.

Similarly, remove the turkey wing by cutting through the joint.

Carve the turkey breast, using the fork to keep the bird steady.

Glazed ham

SERVES 12
PREPARATION TIME 10 minutes
COOKING TIME 1 hour 5 minutes plus resting

6 kg (13 lb 8 oz) cooked leg of ham
70 g (2½ oz/½ cup) cloves

ORANGE GLAZE
250 ml (9 fl oz/1 cup) freshly squeezed orange juice
140 g (5 oz/¾ cup) soft brown sugar
1 tablespoon dijon mustard
175 g (6 oz/½ cup) honey
2 teaspoons soy sauce
2 tablespoons Grand Marnier

or

MUSTARD AND REDCURRANT GLAZE
90 g (3¼ oz/⅓ cup) dijon mustard
315 g (11 oz/1 cup) redcurrant jelly
4 garlic cloves, crushed
2 tablespoons oil
2 tablespoons soy sauce

Preheat the oven to 200°C (400°F/Gas 6). Choose your favourite glaze.

To make the orange glaze, combine the orange juice, sugar, mustard, honey, soy sauce and Grand Marnier in a bowl and mix well.

To make the mustard and redcurrant glaze, place the mustard, redcurrant jelly, garlic, oil and soy sauce in a small saucepan over medium heat and cook, stirring occasionally, for 2–3 minutes, or until the jelly has melted. Be careful that the glaze doesn't catch on the base of the pan.

Use a small sharp knife to cut through the rind around the shank of the ham. To remove the rind, run your thumb around the edge of the cut, under the rind, then ease your hand in between the rind and fat and carefully lift the rind from the fat in one piece. (Use the rind to cover the cut ham when storing.)

Score diagonal cuts into the fat at 4 cm (1½ inch) intervals, forming a diamond pattern. Do not cut all the way through to the ham or the fat will fall off during cooking. Spread half the glaze of your choice over the ham with a palette knife or the back of a spoon and press a clove into the centre of each diamond.

Place the ham, fat side up, on a rack in a roasting tin and pour 500 ml (17 fl oz/ 2 cups) water into the roasting tin. Cover the ham and roasting tin securely with greased foil and bake for 30–40 minutes. Remove the ham from the oven and brush or spread the remaining glaze over the ham. Increase the oven temperature to 210°C (415°F/Gas 6–7). Bake, uncovered, for 20 minutes, until the surface is lightly caramelised and the ham is golden brown. Set aside for 15 minutes to rest before carving (see pages 70–71).

Roast turkey with country sage stuffing

- SERVES 6–8
- PREPARATION TIME 45 minutes
- COOKING TIME 2 hours

3 kg (6 lb 12 oz) turkey
2 tablespoons oil
500 ml (17 fl oz/2 cups) chicken stock
2 tablespoons plain (all-purpose) flour

COUNTRY SAGE STUFFING
45 g (1½ oz) butter
1 onion, finely chopped
1 celery stick, sliced
10 large sage leaves, shredded
160 g (5½ oz/2 cups) fresh white breadcrumbs
1½ teaspoons dried sage
4 tablespoons finely chopped flat-leaf (Italian) parsley
2 egg whites, lightly beaten
1 teaspoon salt
½ teaspoon white pepper

Preheat the oven to 180°C (350°F/Gas 4).

Remove the neck and giblets from inside the turkey. Wash the turkey well and pat dry inside and out with paper towels.

To make the stuffing, melt the butter in a small saucepan and cook the onion and celery over medium heat for 3 minutes, or until the onion has softened. Transfer to a bowl and add the sage leaves, breadcrumbs, dried sage, parsley, egg whites, salt and white pepper.

Spoon the stuffing loosely into the turkey cavity. Tuck the wings underneath and join the cavity with a skewer. Tie the legs together. Place on a wire rack in a baking dish. Roast for 2 hours, basting with the combined oil and 125 ml (4 fl oz/½ cup) of the chicken stock. Cover the breast and legs with foil after 1 hour if the turkey is overbrowning. Test by inserting a skewer between the drumstick and thigh. If the turkey is cooked, the juices will run clear. Cover and rest for 15 minutes before carving (see pages 70–71).

To make the gravy, drain off all except 2 tablespoons of pan juices from the baking dish. Place the dish on the stove over low heat, add the flour and stir well. Stir over medium heat until browned. Gradually add the remaining stock, stirring until the gravy boils and thickens. Serve the turkey with gravy and roast vegetables.

NOTE: Do not stuff the turkey until you are ready to cook it. The stuffing can be made ahead of time and frozen for up to a month in an airtight container. If you prefer to cook the stuffing separately, press it into a lightly greased ovenproof dish and bake for about 30 minutes, or until golden brown. Small greased muffin tins can also be used (bake for 15–20 minutes). Alternatively, form the mixture into balls and fry in a little melted butter or oil, over medium heat, until golden brown all over.

Stuffings

CITRUS STUFFING

Heat 1 tablespoon oil in a small pan. Add 2 finely chopped onions and cook until soft, then transfer to a large bowl and leave to cool. Add 400 g (14 oz) sausage mince (meat), 320 g (11¼ oz/4 cups) fresh white breadcrumbs, 2 crushed garlic cloves, 1 tablespoon each of grated lemon and orange rind, and 120 g (4¼ oz/1 cup) finely chopped pecans and mix to combine. Season with salt and pepper and mix well. Suitable for roast turkey or pork.

CASHEW AND HERB STUFFING

Heat 60 g (2¼ oz) butter in a pan, add 1 chopped onion and 2 crushed garlic cloves and cook until golden. Transfer to a large bowl and allow to cool. Add 465 g (1 lb/2½ cups) of cooked brown rice, 185 g (6½ oz/1 cup) chopped dried apricots, 80 g (2¾ oz/½ cup) chopped unsalted cashews, 3 tablespoons chopped parsley, 2 tablespoons chopped mint and 1 tablespoon lemon juice. Season with salt and pepper, to taste. Suitable for roast turkey, pork or duck.

RICE AND FRUIT STUFFING

Place 600 g (1 lb 5 oz/3 cups) cooked long-grain rice, 80 g (2¾ oz/½ cup) toasted pine nuts, 280 g (10 oz/1½ cups) chopped dried apricots, 375 g (13 oz/1½ cups) of chopped prunes, 4 sliced spring onions (scallions), 1 tablespoon of finely grated orange rind, 80 ml (2½ fl oz/⅓ cup) of orange juice, ½ teaspoon salt, a pinch of white pepper and 1 lightly beaten egg in a large bowl and mix to combine. Suitable for roast turkey, pork or duck.

PISTACHIO STUFFING

Heat 2 tablespoons oil in a small pan and cook 5 finely chopped spring onions (scallions) and 2 teaspoons grated fresh ginger for 2 minutes. Add 6 chopped bacon slices and cook for 3–4 minutes. Transfer to a large bowl and allow to cool. Add 350 g (12 oz) minced (ground) pork and veal, 160 g (5½ oz/2 cups) fresh breadcrumbs, 105 g (3 ½ oz/⅓ cup) marmalade, 1 large handful chopped parsley, 1 lightly beaten egg and 150 g (5½ oz/1 cup) pistachio kernels, season with salt and pepper and mix to combine. Suitable for roast turkey or pork.

MUSHROOM AND TOMATO STUFFING

Heat 2 tablespoons oil in a pan. Add 1 finely chopped onion, 3 crushed garlic cloves, 270 g (9½ oz/3 cups) finely sliced button mushrooms and 2 chopped tomatoes and cook for 5 minutes. Remove from the heat. Combine the mushroom mixture with 370 g (12¾ oz/2 cups) cooked white or brown rice, 50 g (1¾ oz/⅓ cup) finely chopped sun-dried tomatoes, 2 tablespoons shredded basil, 35 g (1¼ oz/⅓ cup) freshly grated parmesan cheese, 2 lightly beaten eggs and some salt and pepper in a bowl and mix to combine. Suitable for roast turkey, pork or duck.

RICOTTA AND BACON STUFFING

Fry 4 finely chopped bacon slices in a fry pan until crisp. Remove and set aside. In the same pan, heat 1 tablespoon oil and fry 2 chopped onions and 2 crushed garlic cloves until golden. Combine 500 g (1 lb 2 oz/2 cups) of ricotta, 1 lightly beaten egg, 35 g (1¼ oz/⅓ cup) of freshly grated parmesan cheese, 160 g (5½ oz/2 cups) of fresh breadcrumbs, 1 large handful of chopped parsley, 2 tablespoons chopped chives, 2 tablespoons chopped tarragon, a pinch of nutmeg and the onion and bacon in a large bowl and mix to combine. Suitable for roast turkey or pork.

'Christmas waves a magic wand over this world, and behold, everything is softer and more beautiful.'

NORMAN VINCENT PEALE

Turkey buffe with rice and fruit stuffing

SERVES 6–8
PREPARATION TIME 1 hour
COOKING TIME 2 hours 10 minutes

2.8 kg (6 lb 3 oz) turkey buffe

STUFFING

280 g (10 oz/1½ cups) cooked long-grain rice
3 tablespoons pine nuts, toasted
180 g (6 oz) dried apricots, chopped
250 g (9 oz) chopped prunes
4 spring onions (scallions), sliced
1 tablespoon finely grated orange rind
80 ml (2½ fl oz/⅓ cup) orange juice
1 egg, lightly beaten

GLAZE

125 ml (4 fl oz/½ cup) orange juice
15 g (½ oz) butter
2 teaspoons soft brown sugar

Bone the turkey breast and remove the bone from the wings.

To make the stuffing, combine the rice, pine nuts, apricots, prunes, spring onion, orange rind, juice, ½ teaspoon salt and some white pepper in a bowl. Mix well and stir in the egg.

Lay the turkey flat and spread the stuffing along the centre. Fold the breast inwards and sew the turkey together using a trussing needle and kitchen string. Tuck in the skin at the neck and press the wings in towards the breast. Sew or tie securely with string, or secure well with skewers. Preheat the oven to 180°C (350°F/Gas 4).

To make the glaze, stir the orange juice, butter and sugar together in a small pan. Bring to the boil and stir until the sugar has dissolved. Allow to cool.

Put the turkey on a wire rack in a baking dish. Roast, basting with the glaze, for 1¾–2 hours, or until cooked through. (If the turkey is overbrowning, loosely cover it with foil.) Cover and set aside for 20 minutes before removing the string or skewers. Slice and serve with the remaining glaze.

NOTE: You will need to cook about 100 g (3½ oz/½ cup) of raw long-grain rice for the stuffing.

Roast chicken with bacon and sage stuffing

SERVES 6 PREPARATION TIME 15 minutes
COOKING TIME 1 hour 10 minutes

- 2 x 1.2 kg (2 lb 12 oz) chickens
- 4 bacon slices
- 2 tablespoons oil
- 1 small onion, finely chopped
- 1 tablespoon chopped sage
- 125 g (4½ oz/1½ cups) fresh breadcrumbs
- 1 egg, lightly beaten

WINE GRAVY

- 2 tablespoons plain (all-purpose) flour
- 2 teaspoons worcestershire sauce
- 2 tablespoons red or white wine
- 560 ml (19¼ fl oz/2¼ cups) beef or chicken stock

Preheat the oven to 180°C (350°F/Gas 4). Remove the giblets and any large fat deposits from the chickens. Wipe over and pat dry inside and out with paper towels.

Finely chop two of the bacon slices. Heat half the oil in a small frying pan and cook the onion and the finely chopped bacon until the onion is soft and the bacon is just starting to brown. Transfer to a bowl and cool. Add the chopped sage, breadcrumbs and egg to the onion, season, to taste, and mix lightly. Spoon some stuffing into each chicken cavity.

Fold the wings back and tuck under the chickens. Tie the legs of each chicken together with string. Place the chickens on a rack in a large baking dish, making sure they are not touching, and brush with some of the oil. Pour 250 ml (9 fl oz/1 cup) of water into the baking dish.

Cut the remaining bacon into long, thin strips and lay across the chicken breasts. Brush the bacon with the remaining oil. Bake the chickens for 45–60 minutes, or until the juices run clear when a thigh is pierced with a skewer. Cover and rest while you prepare the gravy.

To make the gravy, discard all but 2 tablespoons of the pan juices from the baking dish you cooked the chickens in. Heat the dish on the stovetop over medium heat, stir in the flour and cook, stirring, until well browned. Remove from the heat and gradually add the worcestershire sauce, wine and stock. Return to the heat, stir until the mixture boils and thickens, then simmer for 2 minutes. Season, to taste.

Carve the chickens and serve with the wine gravy and some roast vegetables.

Chicken ballottine

SERVES 8 PREPARATION TIME 40 minutes plus refrigeration
COOKING TIME 1 hour 45 minutes

- 1.6 kg (3 lb 8 oz) chicken
- 2 red capsicums (peppers)
- 1 kg (2 lb 4 oz) silverbeet (Swiss chard)
- 30 g (1 oz) butter
- 1 onion, finely chopped
- 1 garlic clove, crushed
- 50 g (1¾ oz/½ cup) grated parmesan cheese
- 80 g (2¾ oz/1 cup) fresh breadcrumbs
- 1 tablespoon chopped oregano
- 200 g (7 oz) ricotta

To bone the chicken, cut through the skin on the centre back with a sharp knife. Separate the flesh from the bone down one side to the breast, without piercing the skin. Follow along the bones with the knife, gradually easing the meat from the thigh, drumstick and wing. Cut through the thigh bone where it meets the drumstick and cut off the wing tip. Repeat on the other side, then lift the rib cage away, leaving the flesh in one piece and the drumsticks still attached to the flesh. Scrape all the meat from the drumstick and wings, discarding the bones. Turn the wing and drumstick flesh inside the chicken and lay the chicken out flat, skin side down. Refrigerate.

Preheat the oven to 180°C (350°F/Gas 4).

Cut the capsicums into large flattish pices, discarding the membranes and seeds. Cook, skin side up, under a hot grill (broiler) until the skins blister and blacken. Cool in a plastic bag, then peel.

Discard the silverbeet stalks and finely shred the leaves. Melt the butter in a large frying pan and cook the onion and garlic over medium heat for 5 minutes, until soft. Add the silverbeet and stir until wilted and the moisture has evaporated. Cool. In a food processor, process the silverbeet and onion mixture with the parmesan, breadcrumbs, oregano and half of the ricotta. Season with salt and pepper.

Spread the silverbeet mixture over the chicken and arrange the capsicum pieces over the top. Form the remaining ricotta into a long roll and place it across the width of the chicken. Fold the sides of the chicken in and over all of the filling so that they overlap slightly. Tuck the ends in neatly. Secure the chicken with toothpicks, then tie it with string at 3 cm (1¼ inch) intervals.

Grease a large piece of foil and place the chicken in the centre. Roll the chicken up securely in the foil, sealing the ends well. Bake on a baking tray for 1¼–1½ hours, or until the juices run clear when a skewer is inserted in the centre of the meat. Cool, then refrigerate until cold.

Remove the foil, toothpicks and string, and cut the chicken into 1 cm (½ inch) slices to serve.

Roast goose with orange and raisin sauce

SERVES 4–6
PREPARATION TIME 30 minutes
COOKING TIME 2 hours

3 kg (6 lb 12 oz) goose
3 tablespoons olive oil
1 onion, roughly chopped
2 garlic cloves, crushed
1 celery stalk, finely chopped
2 tablespoons roughly chopped rosemary
120 g (4¼ oz/1½ cups) fresh white breadcrumbs
finely grated zest of 1 orange
1½ tablespoons orange juice
1 cinnamon stick
2 teaspoons sea salt

ORANGE AND RAISIN SAUCE
2 French shallots, finely chopped
125 ml (4 fl oz/½ cup) dry white wine
125 ml (4 fl oz/½ cup) chicken stock
250 ml (9 fl oz/1 cup) freshly squeezed orange juice
40 g (1½ oz/⅓ cup) raisins

Preheat the oven to 160°C (315°F/Gas 2–3).

Remove any innards from the goose and discard. Rinse the goose inside and out and pat dry with paper towel.

Heat 2 tablespoons of the olive oil in a frying pan over medium heat, add the onion and cook, stirring occasionally, for 3–4 minutes, or until softened. Add the garlic, celery and rosemary and cook, stirring, for 1 minute. Transfer to a large bowl, add the breadcrumbs, orange zest and juice and cinnamon stick, stir to combine, then set aside to cool. Once cool, stuff into the cavity of the goose. Carefully prick the skin all over with a fine skewer and use the skewer to seal the cavity.

Rub the goose with the remaining oil and the sea salt. Place, breast side up, on a rack in a large roasting tin. Roast for 1 hour, basting at 20-minute intervals with the juices that have accumulated in the tin. Increase the temperature to 210°C (415°F/Gas 6–7) and roast the goose for a further 40 minutes, or until the juices run clear when the thigh is pierced with a skewer. Remove the goose from the tin and rest in a warm place for 10 minutes.

To make the orange and raisin sauce, spoon off the fat from the roasting tin and reserve the pan juices. Scrape any drippings from the roasting tin into a saucepan and place over medium heat. Add the shallot and cook, stirring occasionally, for 2–3 minutes. Stir in the wine and simmer until reduced by three-quarters. Add the reserved pan juices and chicken stock and simmer for 8–10 minutes, or until reduced by half. Pour in the orange juice and cook until syrupy. Reduce the heat, add the raisins and simmer for 1–2 minutes, or until the raisins are softened and swollen. Season with sea salt and freshly ground black pepper, and strain.

Carve the goose and serve with the orange and raisin sauce.

Spatchcocks with marmalade and whisky sauce

SERVES 6 PREPARATION TIME 15 minutes
COOKING TIME 1 hour

250 g (9 oz) orange marmalade
2 tablespoons whisky
1 tablespoon dijon mustard
1 orange, cut into 6 wedges
6 small rosemary sprigs
6 spatchcocks (poussins), about 500 g (1 lb 2 oz) each, rinsed and dried, necks trimmed
500 ml (17 fl oz/2 cups) chicken stock

Preheat the oven to 180°C (350°F/Gas 4).

Combine the marmalade, whisky and mustard in a small saucepan. Cook, stirring, over low heat for 5 minutes, until the marmalade is liquid.

Place an orange wedge and a rosemary sprig in the cavity of each spatchcock. Truss with kitchen string and season with sea salt and freshly ground black pepper. Brush two-thirds of the glaze over the spatchcocks.

Put the spatchcocks on a rack in a large roasting tin. Pour half the stock and 125 ml (4 fl oz/1/2 cup) water into the tin. Roast, covering with foil if they are browning too quickly, for 40–45 minutes, until the juices run clear when a skewer is inserted into the thickest part of the flesh. Remove from the oven and set aside to rest in a warm place for 10 minutes.

Pour the roasting juices into a small saucepan. Add the rest of the glaze and stock and simmer for 10 minutes, or until reduced and a sauce-like consistency.

Drizzle the spatchcocks with the sauce. Serve with peas.

Quails with bacon and rosemary

SERVES 4 PREPARATION TIME 30 minutes
COOKING TIME 35 minutes

- 8 quails
- 1 onion, chopped
- 3 bacon slices, chopped
- 1 tablespoon rosemary leaves
- 30 g (1 oz) butter, melted
- 125 ml (4 fl oz/½ cup) port
- 125 ml (4 fl oz/½ cup) cream
- 1 teaspoon cornflour (cornstarch)

Preheat the oven to 200°C (400°F/Gas 6). Wash the quails thoroughly under cold running water, then dry inside and out with paper towels. Tuck the wings underneath the quails and tie the legs close to the body with kitchen string.

Spread the onion, bacon and rosemary over the base of a baking dish, and add the quails. Brush the quails with melted butter. Combine the port with 3 tablespoons of water, then pour 125 ml (½ cup/4 fl oz) of this mixture over the quails.

Bake for about 25 minutes, or until the juices run clear when the quails are pierced in the thigh with a skewer. Cover and leave for 10 minutes in a warm place.

Carefully strain any juices from the baking dish into a small saucepan, reserving the rosemary and bacon mixture. Add the remaining port and water mixture to the pan, and bring to the boil. Reduce the heat and gradually stir in the blended cream and cornflour, stirring until the mixture boils and is slightly thickened. Serve the quails with the sauce and the reserved rosemary and bacon mixture.

NOTE: This recipe can also be made with chicken thigh cutlets instead of quails.

Pork with apple and prune stuffing

SERVES 8
PREPARATION TIME 35 minutes
COOKING TIME 2 hours

- 1 green apple, chopped
- 90 g (3¼ oz/⅓ cup) pitted prunes, chopped
- 2 tablespoons port
- 1 tablespoon chopped flat-leaf (Italian) parsley
- 2 kg (4 lb 8 oz) piece boned pork loin
- olive oil and salt, to rub on pork

GRAVY WITH WINE

- 2 tablespoons plain (all-purpose) flour
- 560 ml (19¼ fl oz/2¼ cups) beef or chicken stock
- 2 tablespoons red or white wine
- 2 teaspoons worcestershire sauce

Preheat the oven to 240°C (475°F/Gas 8).

To make the stuffing, combine the apple, prune, port and parsley. Lay the pork on a board with the rind underneath. Spread the stuffing over the meat side of the loin, roll up and secure with skewers or string at regular intervals. If some of the stuffing falls out while tying, carefully push it back in. Score the pork rind with a sharp knife at 1 cm (½ inch) intervals (if the butcher hasn't already done so) and rub generously with oil and salt.

Place the pork on a rack in a baking dish. Bake for 15 minutes, then reduce the heat to 180°C (350°F/Gas 4) and bake for 1½–2 hours, or until cooked through. The juices will run clear when a skewer is inserted into the thickest part of the meat. Cover and stand for 15 minutes before removing the skewers or string and carving. Reserve any pan juices for making the gravy.

To make the gravy, discard all but 2 tablespoons of the pan juices from the baking dish. Heat the dish on the stovetop over medium heat, stir in the flour and cook, stirring, until well browned. Remove from the heat and gradually add stock, wine and worcestershire sauce. Return to the heat and stir until the mixture boils and thickens, then simmer for 2 minutes. Season with salt and pepper, to taste.

NOTE: If the rind fails to crackle, remove it from the meat, cutting between the fat layer and the meat. Scrape off any excess fat and put the rind on a piece of foil. Cook under a hot grill (broiler) until the rind has crackled. Alternatively, place between several sheets of paper towel and microwave on high in 1 minute bursts, for about 2–3 minutes altogether (depending on the thickness of the rind).

Roast leg of pork

SERVES 6–8 PREPARATION TIME 30 minutes
COOKING TIME 3 hours 25 minutes

4 kg (9 lb) leg of pork
oil and salt, to rub on pork

GRAVY
1 tablespoon brandy or Calvados
2 tablespoons plain (all-purpose) flour
375 ml (13 fl oz/1½ cups) chicken stock
125 ml (4 fl oz/½ cup) unsweetened apple juice

Preheat the oven to 250°C (500°F/Gas 10). Score the pork rind with a sharp knife at 2 cm (¾ inch) intervals. Rub in oil and salt to ensure a crisp crackling. Place the pork, with the rind uppermost, on a rack in a large baking dish. Add a little water to the dish.

Bake for 30 minutes, or until the rind begins to crackle and bubble. Reduce the heat to 180°C (350°F/Gas 4) and then bake for another 2 hours 40 minutes (20 minutes for every 500 g/1 lb 2 oz). The pork is cooked if the juices run clear when the flesh is pierced with a fork. Leave in a warm place for 10 minutes, without covering, before carving.

To make the gravy, drain off all but 2 tablespoons of the pan juices from the baking dish. Place the dish on top of the stove over medium heat, add the brandy and stir quickly to lift the sticky juices from the bottom of the pan. Cook for 1 minute. Remove from the heat, stir in the flour and mix well. Return the pan to the heat and cook, stirring constantly, for another 2 minutes. Remove from the heat, gradually stir in the stock and apple juice, then return to the heat and cook, stirring, until the gravy boils and thickens. Season, to taste, with salt and pepper. Slice the pork and serve with the gravy and some apple sauce (see page 116) and roast vegetables.

NOTE: Cook the pork just before serving. Cover and refrigerate leftover pork for 3–4 days.

Beef Wellington

- SERVES 6–8
- PREPARATION TIME 25 minutes
- COOKING TIME 1 hour 30 minutes

1.2 kg (2 lb 12 oz) beef fillet or rib-eye in 1 piece
1 tablespoon oil
125 g (4½ oz) pâté
60 g (2¼ oz) button mushrooms, sliced
375 g (13 oz) block puff pastry, thawed
1 egg, lightly beaten
1 sheet ready-rolled puff pastry, thawed

Preheat the oven to 210°C (415°F/Gas 6–7). Trim the meat of any excess fat and sinew. Fold the thinner part of the tail end under the meat and tie securely with kitchen string at regular intervals to form an even shape.

Rub the meat with freshly ground black pepper. Heat the oil in a large frying pan over high heat. Add the meat and brown well all over. Remove from the heat and allow to cool. Remove the string.

Spread the pâté over the top and sides of the beef. Cover with the mushrooms, pressing them onto the pâté. Roll out the block pastry on a lightly floured surface to a rectangle large enough to completely enclose the beef.

Place the beef on the pastry, brush the edges with egg, and fold over to completely enclose the meat, brushing the edges of the pastry with the beaten egg to seal, and folding in the ends. Invert onto a greased baking tray so the seam is underneath. Cut leaf shapes from the sheet of puff pastry and use to decorate the Wellington. Use the egg to stick on the shapes. Cut a few slits in the top to allow the steam to escape. Brush the top and sides of the pastry with the egg. Cook for 45 minutes for rare, 1 hour for medium or 1½ hours for well done. Leave in a warm place for 10 minutes before cutting into slices for serving.

NOTE: Use a firm pâté, discarding any jelly. Cover the pastry loosely with foil if it begins to darken too much.

Roast beef with Yorkshire puddings

- SERVES 6
- PREPARATION TIME 15 minutes plus 1 hour refrigeration
- COOKING TIME 1 hour 40 minutes

2 kg (4 lb 8 oz) piece roasting beef (scotch fillet, rump or sirloin)
2 garlic cloves, crushed
oil, for drizzling

YORKSHIRE PUDDINGS

90 g (3¼ oz/¾ cup) plain (all-purpose) flour
125 ml (4 fl oz/½ cup) milk
2 eggs

RED WINE GRAVY

2 tablespoons plain (all-purpose) flour
80 ml (2½ fl oz/⅓ cup) red wine
600 ml (21 fl oz) beef stock

Preheat the oven to 240°C (475°F/Gas 9). Rub the piece of beef with the crushed garlic and some freshly cracked black pepper and drizzle with oil. Bake on a rack in a baking dish for 20 minutes.

Meanwhile, to make the Yorkshire puddings, sift the flour and ½ teaspoon of salt into a bowl, then make a well in the centre and whisk in the milk. In a separate bowl, whisk the eggs together until fluffy, then add to the batter and mix well. Add 125 ml (4 fl oz/½ cup) water and whisk until large bubbles form on the surface. Cover the bowl with plastic wrap and refrigerate for 1 hour.

Reduce the oven to 180°C (350°F/Gas 4) and continue to roast the meat for 1 hour for rare, or longer for well done. Cover loosely with foil and set aside in a warm place while making the Yorkshire puddings.

Increase the oven to 220°C (425°F/Gas 7). Pour off all the pan juices and spoon ½ teaspoon of the juices into twelve 80 ml (2½ fl oz/⅓ cup) patty or muffin tins. (Reserve the remaining juice for the gravy.) Heat the muffin tins in the oven until the fat is almost smoking. Whisk the batter until bubbles form on the surface. Pour into each muffin tin to three-quarters full. Bake for 20 minutes, or until puffed and lightly golden. Make the gravy while the Yorkshire puddings are baking.

To make the gravy, heat 2 tablespoons of the pan juices in the baking dish on the stovetop over low heat. Add the flour and stir well, scraping the dish to incorporate all the sediment. Cook over medium heat for 1–2 minutes, stirring constantly, until the gravy boils and thickens. Simmer for 3 minutes, then season, to taste, with salt and freshly ground black pepper. Strain, if desired.

Serve the roast beef with the hot Yorkshire puddings and red wine gravy.

Barbecued seafood platter

SERVES 6
PREPARATION TIME 40 minutes
COOKING TIME 30 minutes

6 balmain bugs or slipper lobsters
30 g (1 oz) butter, melted
1 tablespoon oil
12 black mussels
12 scallops on their shells
12 oysters
18 raw large prawns (shrimp)

SALSA VERDE
1 tablespoon chopped preserved lemon
1 large handful flat-leaf (Italian) parsley
1 tablespoon drained bottled capers
1 tablespoon lemon juice
3 tablespoons oil

VINEGAR SHALLOT DRESSING
3 tablespoons white wine vinegar
4 French shallots, finely chopped
1 tablespoon chopped chervil

GINGER WASABI SAUCE
1 teaspoon soy sauce
3 tablespoons mirin
2 tablespoons rice wine vinegar
¼ teaspoon wasabi paste
2 tablespoons finely sliced pickled ginger

SWEET BALSAMIC DRESSING
1 tablespoon olive oil
1 tablespoon honey
125 ml (4 fl oz/½ cup) balsamic vinegar

THAI CORIANDER SAUCE
125 ml (4 fl oz/½ cup) sweet chilli sauce
1 tablespoon lime juice
2 tablespoons chopped coriander (cilantro)

Freeze the bugs for 1 hour to immobilize. Cut each bug in half with a sharp knife, then brush the flesh with the combined butter and oil. Set aside while you prepare the rest of the seafood.

Scrub the mussels with a stiff brush and pull out the hairy beards. Discard any mussels that are broken, or any that are open and don't close when tapped on the bench. Rinse well.

Pull off any vein, membrane or hard white muscle from the scallops, leaving any roe attached. Brush the scallops with the combined butter and oil. Cook them, shell side down, on the barbecue.

Remove the oysters from the shells, then rinse the shells under cold water. Pat the shells dry and return the oysters to their shells. Cover and refrigerate the seafood while you make the dressings.

To make the salsa verde, combine all the ingredients in a food processor and process in short bursts until chopped. Transfer to a bowl and add enough oil to moisten the mixture. Season. Serve a dollop on each scallop.

To make the vinegar shallot dressing, whisk the vinegar, shallot and chervil in a bowl until combined. Pour over the cooked mussels.

To make the ginger wasabi sauce, whisk all the ingredients in a small bowl until combined. Spoon over the cooked oysters.

To make the sweet balsamic dressing, heat the olive oil in a pan, add the honey and vinegar and bring to the boil, then boil until reduced by half. Drizzle over the cooked bugs.

To make the Thai coriander sauce, combine all the ingredients in a jug or bowl and drizzle over the cooked prawns.

Cook the seafood on a preheated barbecue grill and flatplate. The mussels, scallops, oysters and prawns all take about 2–5 minutes to cook. The bugs are cooked when the flesh turns white and starts to come away from the shells.

Herbed rack of veal

SERVES 4–6 PREPARATION TIME 45 minutes
COOKING TIME 1 hour 40 minutes

- 1.2 kg (2 lb 12 oz) rack of veal (8 cutlets)
- 80 g (2¾ oz/1 cup) fresh breadcrumbs
- 50 g (1¾ oz/½ cup) dry breadcrumbs
- 1 tablespoon chopped flat-leaf (Italian) parsley
- 1 tablespoon chopped basil
- 2 egg whites, lightly beaten
- 2 garlic cloves, crushed
- 1 tablespoon oil
- 30 g (1 oz) butter, melted

LEMON SAUCE

- 80 ml (2½ fl oz/⅓ cup) dry white wine
- 2 tablespoons lemon juice
- 2 teaspoons sugar
- 125 ml (4 fl oz/½ cup) cream
- 60 g (2¼ oz) chilled butter, cubed
- 1 tablespoon chopped flat-leaf (Italian) parsley

Preheat the oven to 160°C (315°F/Gas 2–3).

Trim the veal of excess fat. Combine all the breadcrumbs, parsley and basil in a bowl. Add the combined egg whites, garlic, oil and butter, and mix. Press the mixture firmly over the meat and place in a baking dish, crust side up. Bake for 1¼ hours for medium, or 1½ hours for well done.

Remove the meat from the pan and leave for 10 minutes. Drain off all except 2 tablespoons of pan juices.

To make the sauce, put the baking dish with the reserved pan juices on the stovetop. Add 125 ml (4 fl oz/½ cup) of water with the wine, lemon juice, sugar and cream. Bring to the boil, then reduce the heat and simmer for 5–7 minutes, until the mixture is reduced by about 125 ml (4 fl oz/½ cup). Remove the dish from the heat and whisk in the butter, one cube at a time, then strain and stir in the parsley. Cut the veal rack into cutlets and serve with the lemon sauce.

Roast leg of lamb with garlic and rosemary

SERVES 6 PREPARATION TIME 20 minutes
COOKING TIME 1 hour 30 minutes

2 kg (4 lb 8 oz) leg of lamb
2 garlic cloves, cut into thin slivers
2 tablespoons rosemary sprigs
2 teaspoons oil

Preheat the oven to moderate 180°C (350°F/Gas 4). Using a small sharp knife, cut small slits all over the lamb. Insert the slivers of garlic and sprigs of rosemary into the slits.

Brush the lamb with the oil and sprinkle with salt and freshly ground black pepper. Place the lamb on a wire rack in a baking dish. Add 125 ml (4 fl oz/1/2 cup) water to the dish and bake for 1 1/2 hours for medium, or until cooked as desired, basting with the pan juices during cooking. Cover the lamb and set aside for 10–15 minutes before carving. Delicious with mint sauce (see page 117).

Tomato and chilli relish

MAKES 1 litre (35 fl oz/4 cups) PREPARATION TIME 20 minutes COOKING TIME 2 hours 20 minutes

8 (900 g/2 lb) tomatoes
3 green apples, peeled, cored and grated
2 onions, chopped
1 teaspoon grated fresh ginger
4 garlic cloves, chopped
1–2 long red chilies, sliced
230 g (8 oz/1 cup firmly packed) light brown sugar
250 ml (9 fl oz/1 cup) cider vinegar

Cut a cross in the base of each tomato, place in a large bowl, then cover with boiling water and leave for 30 seconds, or until the skins split. Transfer to a bowl of cold water. Peel away the skin, then roughly chop the tomatoes and place in a large saucepan.

Add the remaining ingredients to the saucepan and stir over low heat until all the sugar has dissolved. Bring to the boil, then reduce the heat and simmer, stirring often, for 2–2 1/4 hours, or until the relish has reduced and thickened.

Spoon immediately into clean, warm jars and seal. Turn the jars upside down for 2 minutes, then invert and allow to cool. Label and date. Leave for 1 month before opening to allow the flavours to develop. Store in a cool, dark place for up to 12 months. Refrigerate after opening for up to 6 weeks.

Game pie

SERVES 4–6 PREPARATION TIME 40 minutes plus refrigeration
COOKING TIME 2 hours 30 minutes

- 1 kg (2 lb 4 oz) rabbit, boned, cut into bite-sized pieces
- 1.25 kg (2 lb 12 oz) diced venison
- 3 tablespoons plain (all-purpose) flour
- 2–3 tablespoons oil
- 2 bacon slices, chopped
- 1 onion, sliced into thin wedges
- 2 garlic cloves, crushed
- 150 g (5½ oz) button mushrooms, halved
- 250 ml (9 fl oz/1 cup) red wine
- 250 ml (9 fl oz/1 cup) beef stock
- 3 sprigs thyme
- 2 bay leaves
- 185 g (6½ oz) block puff pastry, thawed
- 1 egg yolk
- 2 tablespoons milk

Lightly coat the rabbit and venison in seasoned flour. Heat the oil in a large saucepan and cook the bacon over medium heat until golden. Remove. Brown the rabbit and venison well, in batches, remove and set aside. Add the onion and garlic to the saucepan and cook until browned.

Return the bacon and meat to the pan. Add the mushrooms, wine, stock, thyme and bay leaves. Bring to the boil, reduce the heat and simmer over low heat, stirring occasionally, for 1½ hours, or until the meat is tender. Transfer to a heatproof bowl. Remove the thyme sprigs and bay leaves. Refrigerate until cold.

Preheat the oven to 200°C (400°F/Gas 6).

Spoon the mixture into a 2 litre (70 fl oz/8 cup) ovenproof dish. Roll out the half block of pastry on a lightly floured surface to about 5 mm (¼ inch) thick. Cut strips the width of the pie dish rim and secure to the dish with a little water. Reserve the leftover pastry. Roll the other block of pastry on a lightly floured surface until it is large enough to fit the top of the pie dish. Brush the edges of the pastry strips with a little combined egg yolk and milk. Drape the pastry over the rolling pin and lower it onto the top of the pie. Trim off any excess using a sharp knife. Score the edges of the pastry with the back of a knife to seal. Use any leftover pastry to decorate the top. Cut two slits in the top of the pastry and brush all over with the remaining egg and milk mixture. Bake for 30–40 minutes, or until puffed and golden.

Salmon pie

SERVES 4–6 PREPARATION TIME 25 minutes plus refrigeration
COOKING TIME 1 hour

- 60 g (2¼ oz) butter
- 1 onion, finely chopped
- 200 g (7 oz) button mushrooms, sliced
- 2 tablespoons lemon juice
- 200 g (7 oz) cooked poached salmon fillet, broken into small pieces, or 220 g (7 oz) tinned red salmon
- 2 hard-boiled eggs, chopped
- 2 tablespoons chopped dill
- 3 tablespoons chopped flat-leaf (Italian) parsley
- 185 g (6½ oz/1 cup) cooked long-grain brown rice
- 3 tablespoons cream
- 375 g (13 oz) block puff pastry, thawed
- 1 egg, lightly beaten
- sour cream, to serve (optional)

Melt half the butter in a frying pan and cook the onion for 5 minutes, or until soft but not brown. Add the mushroom and cook for 5 minutes. Stir in the lemon juice, then remove from the pan.

Melt the remaining butter in the pan, add the salmon and stir for 2 minutes. Remove from the heat, cool slightly and add the egg, dill, parsley, and salt and pepper, to taste. Mix gently and set aside. Mix the rice and cream in a small bowl.

Roll out half the pastry to 15 x 25 cm (6 x 10 inches). Neatly trim the pastry, saving the trimmings, and put on a greased baking tray.

Put half the rice into the centre of the pastry, leaving a 3 cm (1¼ inch) border, then top with the salmon and egg mixture, followed by the mushroom, then the remaining rice. Brush the border with egg.

Roll out the other pastry half to 20 x 30 cm (8 x 12 inches) and gently place over the filling. Seal the edges and make two slits in the top. Decorate with the trimmings and chill for 30 minutes.

Preheat the oven to 200°C (400°F/Gas 6). Brush the pie with egg and bake for 15 minutes. Reduce the oven to 180°C (350°F/Gas 4) and bake the pie for another 25–30 minutes, or until crisp and golden. Serve with sour cream.

NOTE: You will need to cook about 100 g (3½ oz/½ cup) of brown rice for this recipe.

Barbecued seafood platter

SERVES 6
PREPARATION TIME 40 minutes
COOKING TIME 30 minutes

6 balmain bugs or slipper lobsters
30 g (1 oz) butter, melted
1 tablespoon oil
12 black mussels
12 scallops on their shells
12 oysters
18 raw large prawns (shrimp)

SALSA VERDE
1 tablespoon chopped preserved lemon
1 large handful flat-leaf (Italian) parsley
1 tablespoon drained bottled capers
1 tablespoon lemon juice
3 tablespoons oil

VINEGAR SHALLOT DRESSING
3 tablespoons white wine vinegar
4 French shallots, finely chopped
1 tablespoon chopped chervil

GINGER WASABI SAUCE
1 teaspoon soy sauce
3 tablespoons mirin
2 tablespoons rice wine vinegar
¼ teaspoon wasabi paste
2 tablespoons finely sliced pickled ginger

SWEET BALSAMIC DRESSING
1 tablespoon olive oil
1 tablespoon honey
125 ml (4 fl oz/½ cup) balsamic vinegar

THAI CORIANDER SAUCE
125 ml (4 fl oz/½ cup) sweet chilli sauce
1 tablespoon lime juice
2 tablespoons chopped coriander (cilantro)

Freeze the bugs for 1 hour to immobilize. Cut each bug in half with a sharp knife, then brush the flesh with the combined butter and oil. Set aside while you prepare the rest of the seafood.

Scrub the mussels with a stiff brush and pull out the hairy beards. Discard any mussels that are broken, or any that are open and don't close when tapped on the bench. Rinse well.

Pull off any vein, membrane or hard white muscle from the scallops, leaving any roe attached. Brush the scallops with the combined butter and oil. Cook them, shell side down, on the barbecue.

Remove the oysters from the shells, then rinse the shells under cold water. Pat the shells dry and return the oysters to their shells. Cover and refrigerate the seafood while you make the dressings.

To make the salsa verde, combine all the ingredients in a food processor and process in short bursts until chopped. Transfer to a bowl and add enough oil to moisten the mixture. Season. Serve a dollop on each scallop.

To make the vinegar shallot dressing, whisk the vinegar, shallot and chervil in a bowl until combined. Pour over the cooked mussels.

To make the ginger wasabi sauce, whisk all the ingredients in a small bowl until combined. Spoon over the cooked oysters.

To make the sweet balsamic dressing, heat the olive oil in a pan, add the honey and vinegar and bring to the boil, then boil until reduced by half. Drizzle over the cooked bugs.

To make the Thai coriander sauce, combine all the ingredients in a jug or bowl and drizzle over the cooked prawns.

Cook the seafood on a preheated barbecue grill and flatplate. The mussels, scallops, oysters and prawns all take about 2–5 minutes to cook. The bugs are cooked when the flesh turns white and starts to come away from the shells.

Lobster with parsley mayonnaise

SERVES 4 PREPARATION TIME 25 minutes
COOKING TIME nil

2 cooked rock lobsters
mixed lettuce leaves, lemon wedges and snipped chives, to serve

PARSLEY MAYONNAISE
40 g (1½ oz) parsley sprigs, stalks removed, finely chopped
3 teaspoons dijon mustard
1 teaspoon honey
1 tablespoon lemon juice
3 tablespoons cream
3 tablespoons mayonnaise

Cut each lobster in half lengthways through the shell. Lift the meat from the tail and body. Crack the legs and prise the meat from them. Remove the cream-coloured vein and soft body matter and discard.

Cut the lobster meat into 2 cm (3/4 inch) pieces, cover and refrigerate.

To make the parsley mayonnaise, put the parsley, mustard, honey, lemon juice, cream and mayonnaise in the bowl of a food processor. Blend until combined, then season. Spoon the mixture into a bowl, cover and refrigerate.

Place a bed of lettuce on each serving plate, top with slices of lobster and spoon parsley mayonnaise over the top.

Poached ocean trout

SERVES 8–10 PREPARATION TIME 50 minutes
COOKING TIME 50 minutes

- 2 litres (70 fl oz/8 cups) good-quality white wine
- 3 tablespoons white wine vinegar
- 2 onions
- 10 cloves
- 4 carrots, chopped
- 1 lemon, cut in quarters
- 2 bay leaves
- 4 parsley sprigs
- 1 teaspoon black peppercorns
- 2.5 kg (5 lb 8 oz) ocean trout, cleaned, gutted and scaled
- lemon slices, to serve

DILL MAYONNAISE

- 1 egg, at room temperature
- 1 egg yolk, at room temperature
- 1 tablespoon lemon juice
- 1 teaspoon white wine vinegar
- 375 ml (13 fl oz/1½ cups) light olive oil
- 1–2 tablespoons chopped dill

Combine the wine and vinegar with 2.5 litres (84 fl oz) water in a large heavy-based saucepan. Stud the onions with the cloves. Add to the pan with the carrot, lemon quarters, bay leaves, parsley and peppercorns. Bring to the boil, reduce the heat and simmer for 30–35 minutes. Cool. Strain into a fish kettle that will hold the trout.

Place the fish in the fish kettle and add water if necessary, to just cover the fish. Bring to the boil, then reduce the heat to a low simmer, cover and poach gently for 10–15 minutes, until the fish flakes when tested in the thickest part. Remove the kettle from the heat and leave the fish to cool in the liquid.

For the dill mayonnaise, process the egg, egg yolk, lemon juice and vinegar in a food processor for 10 seconds, or until blended. With the motor running, add the oil in a thin, steady stream, blending until all the oil is added and the mayonnaise is thick and creamy—it should be thick enough to form peaks. Transfer to a bowl, stir in the dill and season, to taste.

Remove the cold fish from the liquid, place on a serving platter and peel back the skin. Garnish with lemon slices. Serve with the dill mayonnaise.

NOTE: Atlantic salmon, snapper, sea bass or red emperor can also be used. If you don't have a fish kettle, use a baking dish large enough to hold the fish, cover and bake in a 180°C (350°F/Gas 4) oven for 20–30 minutes.

Seafood pie

SERVES 8
PREPARATION TIME 20 minutes
COOKING TIME 1 hour 20 minutes

2 tablespoons olive oil
3 large onions, thinly sliced
1 fennel bulb, thinly sliced
600 ml (21 fl oz) fish stock
750 ml (26 fl oz/3 cups) cream
1 tablespoon brandy
750 g (1 lb 10 oz) skinless snapper fillets, cut into large pieces
250 g (9 oz) scallops
500 g (1 lb 2 oz) raw prawns (shrimp), peeled and deveined
2 tablespoons chopped flat-leaf (Italian) parsley
2 sheets ready-rolled puff pastry, thawed
1 egg, lightly beaten

Preheat the oven to 220°C (425°F/Gas 7). Heat the olive oil in a deep frying pan, add the onion and fennel and cook over medium heat for 20 minutes, or until caramelised.

Add the stock to the pan and bring to the boil. Cook until the liquid is almost evaporated. Stir in the cream and the brandy, bring to the boil, then reduce the heat and simmer for 10 minutes, or until reduced by half.

Add the seafood and parsley and toss for 3 minutes.

Lightly grease a 2.5 litre (84 fl oz) pie dish and add the seafood mixture. Arrange the pastry over the top to cover, trim the excess and then press down around the edges. Decorate the top with any trimmings. Make a steam hole in the top and brush the pastry with the egg. Bake for 30 minutes, or until the filling is cooked and the pastry is crisp and golden.

Blue cheese and onion flan

SERVES 8 PREPARATION TIME 40 minutes plus 40 minutes refrigeration COOKING TIME 1 hour 40 minutes

2 tablespoons olive oil
1 kg (2 lb 4 oz) red onions, very thinly sliced
1 teaspoon soft brown sugar
185 g (6½ oz/1½ cups oz) plain (all-purpose) flour
100 g (3½ oz) cold butter, cubed
185 ml (6 fl oz/¾ cup) cream
3 eggs
100 g (3½ oz) blue cheese, crumbled
1 teaspoon chopped thyme

Heat the olive oil in a heavy-based frying pan over low heat and cook the onion and sugar, stirring, for 45 minutes, or until the onion is caramelised.

Sift the flour into a large bowl. Rub in the butter with your fingertips until the mixture resembles fine breadcrumbs. Make a well in the centre and add 3–4 tablespoons of cold water. Mix with a flat-bladed knife, using a cutting action, until the mixture comes together in beads. Gently gather together and lift onto a lightly floured work surface. Press the pastry into a ball, wrap in plastic wrap and refrigerate for 30 minutes.

Preheat the oven to 180°C (350°F/Gas 4). Lightly grease a 22 cm (8¾ inch) loose-based flan tin. Roll out the pastry on a lightly floured surface to fit the tin. Invert the pastry over the tin and press in with a small ball of pastry, allowing the excess to hang over the side. Trim the excess pastry, then chill for 10 minutes. Line the pastry shell with baking paper and fill with baking beads or uncooked rice. Bake on a baking tray for 10 minutes. Remove the beads and paper, then bake for 10 minutes, or until lightly golden and dry.

Allow the pastry to cool, then gently spread the onion over the base. Whisk the cream in a bowl with the eggs, cheese, thyme and some pepper. Pour over the onion and bake for 35 minutes, or until firm.

Mushroom nut roast

SERVES 6 PREPARATION TIME 30 minutes
COOKING TIME 1 hour

1 large onion
300 g (10½ oz) cap mushrooms
2 tablespoons olive oil
2 garlic cloves, crushed
200 g (7 oz) cashew nuts
200 g (7 oz) brazil nuts
125 g (4½ oz/1 cup) grated cheddar cheese
3 tablespoons freshly grated parmesan cheese
1 egg, lightly beaten
2 tablespoons snipped chives
80 g (2¾ oz/1 cup) fresh wholemeal (whole-wheat) breadcrumbs
chives, extra, to garnish

TOMATO SAUCE
1 onion
1½ tablespoons olive oil
1 garlic clove, crushed
400 g (14 oz) tinned chopped tomatoes
1 tablespoon tomato paste (concentrated purée)
1 teaspoon caster (superfine) sugar

Grease a 14 x 21 cm (5½ x 8¼ inch) loaf (bar) tin and line the base with baking paper.

Dice the onion and finely chop the mushrooms. Heat the oil in a frying pan and add the onion, garlic and mushrooms. Fry until soft, then cool.

Process the nuts in a food processor until finely chopped, but do not overprocess. Preheat the oven to 180°C (350°F/Gas 4).

Combine the cooled mushroom mixture, chopped nuts, cheddar, parmesan, egg, chives and breadcrumbs in a bowl. Mix well and season to taste. Press into the prepared tin and bake for 45 minutes, or until firm. Set aside for 5 minutes.

Meanwhile, to make the tomato sauce, finely chop the onion. Heat the oliv oil in a saucepan, add the onion and garlic and cook, stirring frequently, for 5 minutes, or until soft but not brown. Stir in the tomato, tomato paste, sugar and 80 ml (2½ fl oz/⅓ cup) water. Simmer gently for 3–5 minutes, until slightly thickened. Season.

Turn out the nut roast and garnish with the extra chives. Serve the tomato sauce with the sliced nut roast.

NOTE: For a variation, you can use a different mixture of nuts and add some seeds. You can use nuts such as pecans, almonds, hazelnuts (without skins) and pine nuts. Suitable seeds include sesame, pumpkin or sunflower seeds.

Mushroom, dill and cream cheese coulibiac

SERVES 4–6
PREPARATION TIME 30 minutes
COOKING TIME 40 minutes

100 g (3½ oz/½ cup) long-grain rice
20 g (¾ oz) butter
1 tablespoon olive oil
500 g (1 lb 2 oz) mushrooms caps, wiped clean and finely chopped
2 garlic cloves, crushed
1 tablespoon snipped chives
250 g (9 oz/1 cup) cream cheese, softened
3 tablespoons finely chopped dill
1 tablespoon drained small capers
2 teaspoons lemon juice
4 sheets frozen puff pastry, partially thawed
1 egg, whisked with 1 tablespoon milk
mixed salad leaves, to serve
tomato relish, to serve

Bring 250 ml (9 fl oz/1 cup) water to the boil in a saucepan over medium–high heat. Add the rice, stir briefly and return to the boil. Cover, reduce the heat to low and cook for 10 minutes,or until the rice is tender and the water is absorbed. Remove from the heat and allow to stand for 10 minutes.

Meanwhile, heat the butter and olive oil in a large non-stick frying pan. Add the mushrooms and garlic and cook, stirring, for 4–5 minutes, until the mushrooms are tender. Remove from the heat and season with sea salt and freshly ground black pepper. Stir in the chives, then set aside to cool.

In a bowl, beat together the cream cheese, dill, capers and lemon juice. Season, to taste, and set aside.

Preheat the oven to 220°C (425°F/Gas 7) and line two large baking trays with baking paper.

Cut each pastry sheet in half. Place four pastry pieces on the baking trays. Divide the rice among the pieces, spreading it evenly and leaving a 3 cm (1¼ inch) border. Spoon the mushroom mixture over the rice, then dot the cream cheese mixture over the mushrooms.

Lightly brush the pastry borders with some of the beaten egg. Place the remaining pastry pieces over each mound to cover, then press the edges together with a fork to seal. Cut three slits in each pastry top to allow the steam to escape, then brush with more egg mixture.

Bake for 20–25 minutes, or until the pastry is puffed, golden and cooked through.

Remove from the oven and allow to stand for 10 minutes before slicing. Serve with mixed salad leaves and tomato relish.

Ham and bean salad

SERVES 6 PREPARATION TIME 30 minutes
COOKING TIME 1 minute

- 200 g (7 oz) green beans
- 200 g (7 oz) sugar snap peas
- 200 g (7 oz) frozen broad (fava) beans
- 200 g (7 oz) sliced ham
- 250 g (9 oz) cherry tomatoes, cut in halves
- 115 g (4 oz/¾ cup) toasted cashews
- 2 tablespoons chopped parsley
- 2 tablespoons chopped chives
- 3 tablespoons olive oil
- 2 tablespoons cider vinegar
- ½ teaspoon sugar
- 2 tablespoons chopped mint

Top and tail the green beans and sugar snap peas, then cut the beans diagonally into short lengths. Put the beans, peas and broad beans in a saucepan of boiling water and cook for 1 minute. Drain and refresh in cold water. Discard the outer skin from the broad beans.

Cut the ham into thin strips and combine in a large bowl with the beans and peas, cherry tomatoes, cashews, parsley and chives.

For the dressing, combine the oil, vinegar, sugar and mint in a screwtop jar, shake, then season, to taste. Pour the dressing over the salad and toss well.

Hash ham cake

SERVES 4–6 PREPARATION TIME 30 minutes plus 1 hour refrigeration COOKING TIME 50 minutes

- 500 g (1 lb 2 oz) floury potatoes, peeled and quartered
- 200 g (7 oz) ham, finely chopped
- 4 spring onions (scallions), finely chopped
- 1 small gherkin, finely chopped
- 2 tablespoons chopped parsley
- 1 egg, lightly beaten
- 50 g (1¾ oz) butter

Boil or steam the potato for 10–15 minutes, until tender (pierce with the point of a small knife—if the potato comes away easily, it is ready). Drain well, then put the potato in a large bowl and mash.

Mix in the ham, spring onion, gherkin, parsley, egg and some freshly ground black pepper. Spread on a plate, cover and refrigerate for at least 1 hour, or overnight, to firm.

Heat 30 g (1 oz) of butter in a 20 cm (8 inch) heavy-based frying pan. Spread the potato over the base of the pan and smooth the surface with the back of a spoon. Cook over moderate heat for 15 minutes, then slide out onto a plate. Add the remaining butter to the pan, carefully flip the cake back into the pan and cook for another 15–20 minutes, or until the outside forms a brown crust. Serve in wedges.

Pea and ham risotto

SERVES 4 PREPARATION TIME 25 minutes
COOKING TIME 45 minutes

- 1 tablespoon olive oil
- 1 celery stick, chopped
- 2 tablespoons chopped flat-leaf (Italian) parsley
- 75 g (2½ oz) ham, chopped
- 250 g (9 oz/1⅔ cups) frozen peas
- 125 ml (4 fl oz/½ cup) dry white wine
- 750 ml (26 fl oz/3 cups) chicken stock
- 60 g (2¼ oz) butter
- 1 onion, chopped
- 440 g (15½ oz/2 cups) risotto rice
- 35 g (1¼ oz/⅓ cup) freshly grated parmesan cheese
- shaved parmesan, for serving

Heat the oil in a frying pan and cook the celery and parsley for 3 minutes. Stir in the ham, peas and half the wine and bring to the boil. Simmer until the liquid has evaporated. Put the stock, remaining wine and 750 ml (26 fl oz/3 cups) water in a separate pan. Keep at simmering point.

Melt the butter in a large saucepan and stir the onion until softened. Stir in the rice. Add 125 ml (4 fl oz/1/2 cup) of the stock, stirring until it is absorbed. Continue adding the stock, 125 ml (4 fl oz/1/2 cup) at a time, stirring, for 20–25 minutes, until the rice is tender and creamy. Season, then add the pea mixture and grated parmesan. Serve with shaved parmesan.

Ham and cider casserole

SERVES 4 PREPARATION TIME 15 minutes
COOKING TIME 25 minutes

- 40 g (1½ oz) butter
- 1 onion, chopped
- 2 leeks, white part only, finely sliced
- 2 garlic cloves, crushed
- 8 slices ham, chopped
- 100 ml (3½ fl oz) apple cider
- 300 g (10½ oz) can butter beans, rinsed and drained
- 25 g (¾ oz/⅓ cup) fresh breadcrumbs
- 1 tablespoon freshly grated parmesan cheese

Preheat the oven to 200°C (400°F/Gas 6). Melt half the butter in a heavy-based frying pan, add the onion and cook over low heat for 2–3 minutes, or until tender. Add the leek and stir until cooked through. Stir in the garlic.

Transfer the onion mixture to an ovenproof dish. Scatter the chopped ham over the top and season with freshly ground black pepper. Pour in the apple cider. Spoon the butter beans over and around the ham and sprinkle with the breadcrumbs and parmesan. Dot with the remaining butter and bake for 20 minutes, or until lightly golden on top.

Turkey empanadas

MAKES 18 PREPARATION TIME 40 minutes
COOKING TIME 25 minutes

- 1 tablespoon oil
- 1 onion, finely chopped
- 1 garlic clove, crushed
- 2 teaspoons paprika
- 1 teaspoon ground cumin
- ½ teaspoon ground cinnamon
- 2 tablespoons sherry
- 400 g (14 oz) can crushed tomatoes
- 400 g (14 oz) cooked turkey, finely chopped
- 110 g (3¾ oz/½ cup) pitted green olives, chopped
- 3 hard-boiled eggs, chopped
- 1 tablespoon chopped parsley
- 4½ sheets ready-rolled shortcrust pastry
- oil, for deep-frying

Heat the oil in a frying pan over medium heat and cook the onion and garlic for 2 minutes. Stir in the paprika, cumin and cinnamon until fragrant. Add the sherry, tomato and turkey. Boil for 10 minutes, or until thickened. Remove from the heat and stir in the olives, egg and parsley. Season, then cool.

Cut the pastry into 12 cm (5 inch) rounds. Put 1½ tablespoons of the mixture on each round, brush the edge with water and fold over to enclose the filling. Seal the edges with a fork.

Deep-fry the empanadas in batches for 2–3 minutes on each side, or until golden brown. Drain on crumpled paper towels.

Turkey potato salad

SERVES 6 PREPARATION TIME 25 minutes
COOKING TIME 15 minutes

- 2 tablespoons oil
- 4 spring onions (scallions), cut into thin strips
- 2 zucchini (courgettes), thickly sliced
- 750 g (1 lb 10 oz) new baby potatoes
- 1 red apple
- 1 tablespoon lemon juice
- 400 g (14 oz) cooked turkey, cut into thin strips
- 2 tablespoons chopped flat-leaf (Italian) parsley

DRESSING

- 125 g (4½ oz/½ cup) whole-egg mayonnaise
- 3 teaspoons Dijon mustard
- 1 tablespoon wholegrain mustard
- 2 tablespoons lemon juice

Heat the oil in a small frying pan and fry the spring onion until crisp. Remove and drain on crumpled paper towels.

Steam or boil the zucchini and potatoes until just tender. Refresh the zucchini in cold water. Cut the cooled potatoes in half. Cut the apple into wedges and toss with the lemon juice.

Combine the dressing ingredients, then season, to taste. Toss the potato, apple, zucchini, turkey and parsley with the dressing until combined. Serve with the crispy spring onion.

Turkey filo parcels

MAKES 24 PREPARATION TIME 35 minutes
COOKING TIME 40 minutes

- 20 g (¾ oz) butter
- 200 g (7 oz) button mushrooms, sliced
- 4 bacon slices, diced
- 350 g (12 oz) cooked turkey, chopped
- 150 g (5½ oz) ricotta
- 2 spring onions (scallions), sliced
- 3 tablespoons shredded basil
- 24 sheets filo pastry
- melted butter, for brushing
- sesame seeds, for sprinkling

Melt the butter in a large saucepan and add the mushrooms and bacon. Cook over high heat for 5 minutes, or until the mushrooms are soft and there is no liquid left. Put the turkey, ricotta, spring onion and basil in a bowl and mix to combine. Add the mushroom mixture, then season, to taste.

Preheat the oven to 180°C (350°F/Gas 4). Layer three sheets of pastry on a work surface, brushing each layer with melted butter. Cut into three strips. Place 1 tablespoon of the filling at the end of each strip and fold the pastry over to form a triangle. Fold until you reach the end of the pastry. Repeat with the remaining pastry and filling. Place the parcels on a greased baking tray, brush with butter and sprinkle with the sesame seeds. Bake for 30–35 minutes, or until golden.

Turkey san choy bau

SERVES 4 PREPARATION TIME 15 minutes plus 15 minutes soaking COOKING TIME 5 minutes

- 8 small iceberg lettuce leaves
- 5 dried Chinese mushrooms
- 100 g (3½ oz) canned baby corn
- 2 spring onions (scallions)
- 1 teaspoon sesame oil
- 2 teaspoons oil
- 2 garlic cloves, crushed
- 1 tablespoon grated fresh ginger
- 100 g (3½ oz) bean sprouts
- 300 g (10½ oz) cooked turkey, finely chopped
- 90 g (3¼ oz/½ cup) water chestnuts, finely chopped
- 1 tablespoon chopped coriander (cilantro)
- 1 teaspoon sugar
- 1 tablespoon oyster sauce
- 1 tablespoon soy sauce

Soak the lettuce leaves in cold water while you prepare the filling. Soak the mushrooms boiling water for 15 minutes, or until soft. Drain, discard the stems and finely chop the caps. Thinly slice the baby corn and chop the spring onions.

Heat the oils in a pan over medium heat, add the garlic, ginger and corn, and toss until fragrant. Add the mushrooms, spring onion, bean sprouts, turkey, water chestnuts, coriander, sugar, oyster sauce and soy sauce. Toss to heat through.

Drain the lettuce and pat dry with paper towels. Spoon some turkey filling into each lettuce cup and serve.

Sauces

These delicious classic sauces and gravies can be quickly made while the roast is cooking or resting. Mint sauce will develop in flavour if made a day in advance.

APPLE SAUCE

Peel, core and roughly chop 4 green apples. Place the apple in a pan with 1 tablespoon caster (superfine) sugar, 125 ml (4 fl oz/1/2 cup) water, 2 cloves and 1 cinnamon stick. Cover and simmer for 10 minutes, or until soft. Remove from the heat and discard the cloves and cinnamon stick. Mash or, for a finer sauce, press through a sieve. Stir in 1–2 teaspoons lemon juice, or to taste. Serve with roast pork or ham. Makes 250 ml (9 fl oz/1 cup).

GRAVY WITH WINE

Discard all but 2 tablespoons of the pan juices from the baking dish you cooked the roast in. Heat the dish on the stovetop over moderate heat, stir in 2 tablespoons plain (all-purpose) flour and cook, stirring, until well browned. Remove from the heat and gradually add 2 teaspoons of worcestershire sauce, 2 tablespoons red or white wine and 560 ml (19 1/4 fl oz/2 1/4 cups) beef or chicken stock. Return to the heat, stir until the mixture boils and thickens, then simmer for 2 minutes. Season with salt and pepper. Suitable for all roast meats. Makes 375 ml (13 fl oz/1 1/2 cups).

MINT SAUCE

Sprinkle 1 tablespoon caster (superfine) sugar over a handful of mint leaves on a chopping board, then finely chop the mint. Transfer to a bowl and add another 2 tablespoons of caster (superfine) sugar. Cover with 3 tablespoons boiling water and stir until the sugar has dissolved. Stir in 185 ml (6 fl oz/3/4 cup) malt vinegar, cover and chill overnight. Traditionally served with roast lamb. Makes 375 ml (13 fl oz/1 1/2 cups).

CREAMY HORSERADISH

Combine 175 g (6 oz) horseradish cream and 1 finely chopped spring onion (scallion) with 3 tablespoons of sour cream in a bowl. Fold in 125 ml (4 fl oz/1/2 cup) of whipped cream and season, to taste. Serve with roast beef or roast veal. Makes 1 1/2 cups (375 ml/12 oz).

BREAD SAUCE

Slice 1 small onion and combine in a small pan with 315 ml (10 3/4 fl oz/1 1/4 cups) milk, 1 bay leaf, 4 black peppercorns and 2 cloves. Bring to the boil over medium heat, then simmer for 10 minutes. Strain into a large heatproof bowl and discard the solids. Add 100 g (3 1/2 oz/1 1/4 cups) of fresh breadcrumbs, a pinch of ground nutmeg and 20 g (3/4 oz) of butter. Stir until smooth, then season, to taste. Traditionally served with roast goose, turkey or chicken. Makes 315 ml (10 3/4 fl oz/1 1/4 cups).

RASPBERRY AND CRANBERRY SAUCE

Purée 150 g (5 1/2 oz) raspberries, then press through a sieve. Combine the purée in a small pan with 3 tablespoons orange juice, 160 g (5 1/2 oz/1/2 cup) cranberry sauce, 2 teaspoons dijon mustard and 1 teaspoon finely grated orange rind. Stir over heat until smooth. Add 3 tablespoons port and simmer for 5 minutes. Cool before serving with roast turkey, goose, ham or duck. Makes 250 ml (9 fl oz/1 cup).

Merry Christmas
Christmas
Seasons Greetings

Sides

Basic potatoes

SERVES 4 PREPARATION TIME 15 minutes
COOKING TIME 55 minutes

- 4 large floury or all-purpose potatoes, such as spunta, sebago, russet, desiree or pontiac, peeled
- 20 g (¾ oz) butter, melted
- 1 tablespoon oil

Preheat the oven to 180°C (350°F/Gas 4). Cut the potatoes in half and simmer in a pan of water for 5 minutes. Drain and cool on paper towels. Using a fork, scrape the rounded side of the potatoes to form a rough surface. Place in a lightly greased baking dish and brush with the melted butter and oil. Roast for 50 minutes, or until golden, brushing halfway through the cooking time with a little more butter and oil.

Orange sweet potato

SERVES 4 PREPARATION TIME 10 minutes
COOKING TIME 25 minutes

- 800 g (1 lb 12 oz) orange sweet potato, peeled
- 20 g (¾ oz) butter, melted
- 2 teaspoons sesame seeds
- ½ teaspoon cracked black pepper

Preheat the oven to 180°C (350°F/Gas 4). Cut the orange sweet potato into 1 cm (½ inch) thick slices. Combine with the butter, sesame seeds and pepper. Toss, then roast in a baking dish for 25 minutes, or until lightly browned and tender, turning once. Sprinkle with salt before serving.

Roast onions

SERVES 6 PREPARATION TIME 20 minutes
COOKING TIME 1 hour 10 minutes

- 6 onions
- 60 g (2¼ oz/¾ cup) fresh breadcrumbs
- 3 tablespoons freshly grated romano or parmesan cheese
- 1 tablespoon chopped basil
- 20 g (¾ oz) butter, melted

Preheat the oven to 180°C (350°F/Gas 4). Peel the onions, leaving the root ends intact. Place in a pan of water, bring to the boil and simmer gently for 20 minutes. Remove and cool. Cut off the top quarter of each onion, and scoop out a third of the inside. Combine the breadcrumbs, cheese, basil and butter and season. Spoon into the onions. Roast in a lightly greased baking dish for 50 minutes, until the onions are soft.

Pancetta potatoes

SERVES 4 PREPARATION TIME 20 minutes
COOKING TIME 50 minutes

- 8 medium floury or all-purpose potatoes, such as sebago, spunta, russet, desiree or pontiac, peeled
- 2 slices pancetta
- 8 rosemary sprigs
- 2 teaspoons butter, softened
- oil, for brushing

Preheat the oven to 180°C (350°F/Gas 4). Trim the bases of the potatoes so they sit flat. Cut each pancetta slice lengthways into 4 pieces. Roll a sprig of rosemary in each piece of pancetta. Cut a hole in the centre of the potatoes about halfway through and insert the pancetta. Place in a greased baking dish. Top each potato with ¼ teaspoon of the butter. Brush with oil and sprinkle with pepper. Roast for 40–50 minutes, or until golden.

NOTE: The texture of potatoes varies from waxy to floury or starchy and it is best to use the type stated in recipes. Sebago and pontiac are good all-rounders and particularly good for baking. Russet and spunta have a floury texture and are also good baking varieties.

Roasted stuffed tomatoes

SERVES 6 PREPARATION TIME 20 minutes
COOKING TIME 25 minutes

- 6 ripe tomatoes
- 20 g (¾ oz) butter
- 2 bacon slices, finely chopped
- 75 g (2½ oz) button mushrooms, finely chopped
- 1 spring onion (scallion), finely chopped
- 80 g (2¾ oz/1 cup) fresh breadcrumbs
- oil, for drizzling

Preheat the oven to 180°C (350°F/Gas 4). Cut the tops off the tomatoes and reserve the tops. Scoop out the seeds and soft flesh. Melt the butter in a frying pan over low heat. Fry the bacon and button mushrooms for 5 minutes, or until soft. Transfer to a bowl. Stir in the spring onion and breadcrumbs and season with salt and freshly ground black pepper. Fill the tomatoes with the mixture and replace the tops. Place on a baking tray and drizzle with oil. Roast for 20 minutes, or until heated through.

Rosemary roasted pumpkin

SERVES 6 PREPARATION TIME 10 minutes
COOKING TIME 30 minutes

- 1.7 kg (3 lb 12 oz) pumpkin (winter squash), such as jap or kent
- 3 tablespoons extra virgin olive oil
- 3 tablespoons roughly chopped rosemary

Preheat the oven to 200°C (400°F/Gas 6). Cut the pumpkin into wedges and remove the seeds, leaving the skin on. Toss in the olive oil and rosemary and season with sea salt. Place in a roasting tin. Roast for 30 minutes, or until the pumpkin is golden and tender.

Roasted balsamic onions

SERVES 8 PREPARATION TIME 10 minutes
COOKING TIME 55 minutes

- 3 tablespoons roughly chopped thyme, plus extra thyme leaves, to garnish
- 2 tablespoons balsamic vinegar
- 1 tablespoon olive oil
- 1 kg (2 lb 4 oz) baby onions, peeled

Preheat the oven to 180°C (350°F/Gas 4). Combine the thyme, balsamic vinegar and olive oil in a large bowl, add the onions and carefully toss to coat. Transfer the onions to a non-stick baking tray and cover with baking paper to prevent the vinegar burning. Roast for 50–55 minutes, turning once or twice, or until the onions are caramelised and soft. Garnish with the extra thyme.

Maple syrup roasted parsnips

SERVES 6 PREPARATION TIME 10 minutes
COOKING TIME 45 minutes

- 700 g (1 lb 9 oz) parsnips, peeled and trimmed
- 30 g (1 oz) butter, chopped
- 1 tablespoon olive oil
- 2 tablespoons pure maple syrup

Preheat the oven to 200°C (400°F/Gas 6). Cut the parsnips into quarters lengthways. Heat the butter and oil in a roasting tin, add the parsnips and toss to coat. Roast for 30 minutes, turning twice. Remove from the oven, drizzle the maple syrup over the parsnips and toss until well coated. Return to the oven to roast for 15 minutes, or until tender and golden.

Sweet potato crumble

SERVES 6 PREPARATION TIME 25 minutes
COOKING TIME 40 minutes

- 1 kg (2 lb 4 oz) orange sweet potato
- 50 g (1¾ oz) butter
- 80 ml (2½ fl oz/⅓ cup) milk or cream
- ¼ teaspoon ground cinnamon
- 480 g (1 lb 1 oz) loaf sourdough bread
- 55 g (2 oz/½ cup) freshly grated parmesan cheese
- 1 teaspoon dried thyme leaves

Preheat the oven to 180°C (350°F/Gas 4). Cut the orange sweet potato into chunks and cook in a saucepan of lightly salted boiling water for 15 minutes, or until tender. Drain and return to the saucepan. Mash with a potato masher, adding the butter, milk and cinnamon. Season with salt and freshly ground black pepper, then spoon the mash into a shallow 1 litre (35 fl oz/4 cup) casserole dish and smooth the top.

Remove the crusts from the bread, break the bread into smaller pieces and finely chop in a food processor. Mix in the parmesan and thyme, then scatter over the mash and bake for 20 minutes, or until the crumble is golden and crispy.

Potato purée

SERVES 6 PREPARATION TIME 10 minutes
COOKING TIME 20 minutes

- 1 kg (2 lb 4 oz) boiling potatoes, peeled and diced
- 200 ml (7 fl oz) cream
- 75 g (2½ oz) butter, softened
- 1 teaspoon sea salt

Cook the potatoes in a saucepan of boiling salted water for 12–14 minutes, or until tender. Drain, return the potatoes to the pan and cook, stirring, over medium heat for 2 minutes to allow any excess moisture to evaporate. Pass the potato through a mouli or roughly mash and push through a sieve, then return to the pan.

Place the cream and butter in a small saucepan and bring almost to boiling point. Pour onto the potato, add the salt and cook, stirring, over low heat until the purée is smooth and warmed through.

Roast vegetable mash

SERVES 4–6 PREPARATION TIME 30 minutes
COOKING TIME 1 hour 30 minutes

- 2 large pontiac or sebago potatoes
- 400 g (14 oz) pumpkin (winter squash)
- 400 g (14 oz) orange sweet potato
- 2 large parsnips
- 1 large onion, chopped
- 2 ripe tomatoes, quartered
- 6 garlic cloves, unpeeled
- 2 tablespoons olive oil
- 30 g (1 oz) butter, chopped

Preheat the oven to 180°C (375°F/Gas 4). Peel the potatoes, pumpkin, sweet potato and parsnip, then cut into large pieces and place in a large baking dish. Add the onion, tomato and garlic. Drizzle with the olive oil and sprinkle with some salt and cracked black pepper.

Bake the vegetables for 1½ hours, or until soft and starting to brown, turning every 30 minutes. Peel the garlic and transfer the vegetables to a bowl. Add the butter and mash. Season, to taste, with salt and freshly ground pepper.

NOTE: You could also substitute swede (rutabaga), celeriac or Jerusalem artichoke for the parsnips, or substitute carrot for the pumpkin or orange sweet potato.

Mustard mash

SERVES 8 PREPARATION TIME 5 minutes
COOKING TIME 1 hour

- 2 kg (4 lb 8 oz) all-purpose potatoes, such as desiree, unpeeled
- 100 g (3½ oz) butter
- 3 tablespoons dijon mustard
- 100 ml (3½ fl oz) cream
- 2 tablespoons sea salt

Preheat the oven to 220°C (425°F/Gas 7). Put the potatoes in a roasting tin and roast for 1 hour, or until very tender when pierced with a small sharp knife. Set aside and allow to cool slightly. When the potatoes are cool enough to handle, peel and place in a large bowl.

Meanwhile, gently heat the butter, mustard and cream in a small saucepan over low heat. Stir until the mixture is melted and combined. Do not boil. Pour over the potato, season with the salt and mash until soft and creamy.

Honey-roasted vegetables

SERVES 4 PREPARATION TIME 20 minutes
COOKING TIME 50 minutes

4 parsnips
2 carrots
2 small orange sweet potatoes
4 beetroot (beets), cut into wedges
8 garlic cloves, unpeeled
3 tablespoons oil
1 tablespoon honey
1 teaspoon cumin seeds
½ teaspoon cracked black pepper
½ teaspoon rock salt

Preheat the oven to 200°C (400°F/Gas 6). Cut the parsnips, carrots and sweet potatoes into 10 cm (4 inch) lengths. Place the vegetables and unpeeled garlic in a large baking dish, and drizzle with the oil and honey. Sprinkle with the cumin seeds, pepper and salt. Toss to coat.

Bake the vegetables for 40–50 minutes, or until tender inside and golden brown outside.

Duchess potatoes

SERVES 6 PREPARATION TIME 20 minutes plus cooling
COOKING TIME 30 minutes

860 g (1 lb 14 oz) floury potatoes, quartered
2 eggs
3 tablespoons cream
2 tablespoons freshly grated parmesan cheese
¼ teaspoon grated nutmeg
1 egg yolk, for glazing

Boil or steam the potato for 10 minutes, or until just tender (pierce with the point of a small knife—if the potato comes away easily, it is ready). Drain, return to the pan and shake over very low heat for 1–2 minutes to dry out the potato. Transfer to a bowl and mash well until smooth.

Beat together the eggs, cream, parmesan and nutmeg with some salt and black pepper. Add to the potato and mash to combine. Taste for seasoning and adjust if necessary. Cover and leave for 20 minutes to cool slightly. Preheat the oven to 180°C (350°F/Gas 4).

Put the just warm potato mixture in a piping (icing) bag fitted with a 1.5 cm (5/8 inch) star nozzle. Pipe the mixture in swirls, not too close together, onto greased baking trays. Lightly brush all over with the egg yolk, to give a golden, crisp finish. Bake for 15–20 minutes, or until golden. Serve hot, sprinkled with a little paprika if desired.

NOTE: These can be prepared in advance and refrigerated, covered with plastic. Just before serving, brush with egg yolk and bake.

Risotto-stuffed onions

SERVES 8 PREPARATION TIME 15 minutes
COOKING TIME 1 hour 40 minutes

8 onions (about 200 g/7 oz each)
1 tablespoon oil
20 g (¾ oz) butter
70 g (2½ oz) mushrooms, chopped
20 g (¾ oz) prosciutto, chopped
110 g (3 ¾ oz/½ cup) arborio rice
625 ml (21½ fl oz/2½ cups) hot chicken stock
2 tablespoons freshly grated parmesan cheese
2 tablespoons chopped parsley

Preheat the oven to 200°C (400°F/Gas 6). Trim the bases of the onions so they sit flat and cut the tops off, leaving a wide opening. Place in a baking dish, drizzle with the oil and bake for 1–1½ hours, or until golden.

Meanwhile, melt the butter in a pan, add the chopped mushrooms and prosciutto and cook for 5 minutes, or until the mushrooms have softened. Add the rice and stir until well coated with the butter. Gradually stir in the hot stock, 125 ml (4 fl oz/½ cup) at a time, making sure the liquid is absorbed before adding more. When all the stock has been used, stir in the parmesan and parsley.

Scoop out the flesh from the middle of each onion, leaving at least 3 outside layers on each, to hold the filling. Chop the scooped flesh and stir through the risotto. Spoon the filling into the onion shells, piling a little on top. Bake the onions for 10 minutes to heat through, then serve.

Spiced red cabbage

SERVES 6 PREPARATION TIME 20 minutes
COOKING TIME 1 hour 30 minutes

- 750 g (1 lb 10 oz) red cabbage
- 1 large red onion, chopped
- 1 green apple, cored and chopped
- 2 garlic cloves, crushed
- 1/4 teaspoon ground cloves
- 1/4 teaspoon ground nutmeg
- 1 1/2 tablespoons soft brown sugar
- 2 tablespoons red wine vinegar
- 20 g (3/4 oz) butter, cubed

Preheat the oven to slow 150°C (300°F/Gas 2). Quarter the cabbage and remove the core. Finely slice the cabbage and put it in a large casserole dish with the onion and red apple. Toss well.

Combine the garlic, spices, sugar and vinegar. Pour over the cabbage, and toss. Dot the top with the butter. Cover and bake for 1 1/2 hours, stirring once or twice. Season with salt and freshly ground black pepper. Serve hot.

Braised fennel

SERVES 8 PREPARATION TIME 15 minutes
COOKING TIME 30 minutes

- 4 small fennel bulbs
- 20 g (3/4 oz) butter
- 1 tablespoon sugar
- 80 ml (2 1/2 fl oz/1/3 cup) white wine
- 160 ml (5 1/4 fl oz/2/3 cup) chicken stock
- 1 tablespoon sour cream

Slice the fennel into quarters, reserving the fronds. Melt the butter in a frying pan and stir in the sugar. Add the fennel and cook for 5–10 minutes, until lightly browned all over.

Pour in the wine and stock and bring to the boil, then reduce the heat and simmer, covered, for 10 minutes, or until tender.

Uncover and boil until most of the liquid has evaporated and the sauce has become sticky. Remove from the heat and stir in the sour cream. Garnish with the reserved fennel fronds.

Herbed carrots

SERVES 6 PREPARATION TIME 15 minutes
COOKING TIME 10 minutes

1 kg (2 lb 4 oz) carrots
40 g (1½ oz) butter
2 teaspoons sugar
2 teaspoons lemon juice
2 teaspoons finely chopped flat-leaf (Italian) parsley

Peel the carrots and cut into thick matchsticks. Cook in a saucepan of boiling water for 3–5 minutes, or until tender. Drain well.

Melt the butter in the saucepan and add the sugar. Return the carrots to the pan and toss together until the carrots start to colour a little. Add the lemon juice and parsley and toss together until the carrots are well coated.

Broccoli with almonds

SERVES 6 PREPARATION TIME 10 minutes
COOKING TIME 10 minutes

500 g (1 lb 2 oz) broccoli, cut into small florets
2 teaspoons oil
20 g (¾ oz) butter
1 garlic clove, crushed
1 tablespoon flaked almonds

Add the broccoli to a saucepan of boiling water and cook for 1–2 minutes, until just tender. Drain thoroughly. Heat the oil and butter in a large frying pan. Cook the garlic and almonds for 1–2 minutes, until the almonds are golden. Remove from the pan and set aside.

Add the broccoli to the frying pan and toss over medium heat for 2–3 minutes, until the broccoli is heated through. Return the almond mixture to the pan and stir until well distributed. Serve hot.

Accompaniments

The flavour of roasts and cold cuts can be transformed by serving them with one of these imaginative concoctions.

BEETROOT RELISH

Put 750 g (1 lb 10 oz) peeled, coarsely grated beetroot (beets) in a large saucepan with 1 chopped onion, 400 g (14 oz) peeled and chopped green apples, 90 g (3 1/4 oz/1/2 cup) soft brown sugar, 125 g (4 1/2 oz/1/2 cup) sugar, 2 tablespoons lemon juice and 2 teaspoons salt. Pour in 420 ml (14 1/2 fl oz/1 2/3 cups) white wine vinegar and stir over low heat, without boiling, until the sugar has dissolved. Bring to the boil and simmer, stirring often, for 20–30 minutes, until the beetroot and onion are tender and the relish is reduced and thickened. Spoon into clean, warm jars and seal. Turn upside down for 2 minutes, invert and leave to cool. Label and date. Leave for a month before using. Store in a cool, dark place for up to 12 months. Refrigerate after opening, for up to 6 weeks. Serve with ham, beef, turkey, duck or goose. Makes 1 litre (35 fl oz/4 cups).

MOSTARDA DI FRUTTA

Blend 1 teaspoon cornflour (cornstarch) with 1 tablespoon water in a small bowl. Pour 185 ml (6 fl oz/3/4 cup) water into a saucepan and pour in 310 ml (10 3/4 fl oz/1 1/4 cups) white wine. Add 1 tablespoon honey, 3 cloves, 1 tablespoon yellow mustard seeds, 1/4 teaspoon ground nutmeg, 1/2 teaspoon freshly grated nutmeg and 2 broken cinnamon sticks. Bring to the boil, then stir in the cornflour mixture, lower the heat and cook, stirring, for 5 minutes, until the mixture boils and thickens. Add 175 g (6 oz) chopped assorted glacé (candied) fruits and 1 tablespoon lemon juice. Simmer for 15 minutes, until the fruit is soft and the mixture is thick. Spoon into a clean, warm jar and seal immediately. Delicious served with cold meats, especially ham, and poultry and game. Makes 250 ml (9 fl oz/1 cup).

GRAINY SWEET MUSTARD

Combine 30 g (1 oz) brown or black mustard seeds with 70 g ($2^1/_2$ oz) yellow mustard seeds. Add 125 ml (4 fl oz/$^1/_2$ cup) of white wine vingar, cover and leave overnight. Process three-quarters of the mustard seed mixture, 2 teaspoons of lemon juice, 1 teaspoon of salt and 1 tablespoon of honey in a food processor until roughly crushed. Transfer to a bowl and stir in the remaining seeds. Spoon into clean jars. Seal. Refrigerate after opening. Keeps for 2 months. Makes 250 g (9 oz/1 cup).

WASABI MAYONNAISE

Combine 125 g ($4^1/_2$ oz/$^1/_2$ cup) each of whole-egg mayonnaise and thick natural yoghurt in a bowl with 2 teaspoons wasabi paste and 1 tablespoon each of freshly squeezed lime juice and chopped fresh coriander (cilantro). Stir until combined, then stand for at least 20 minutes before serving. This mayonnaise is particularly suitable for serving with cold seafood such as oysters, prawns (shrimp) and fish. Makes 250 g (9 oz/1 cup).

RED CAPSICUM AND CORIANDER AIOLI

Drain the oil from 150 g ($5^1/_2$ oz) of chargrilled capsicums (peppers). Process the capsicums in a food processor with 250 g (9 oz/1 cup) whole-egg mayonniase for 2 minutes, or until smooth. Add 1 crushed garlic clove and 1 tablespoon each of lemon juice and chopped fresh coriander (cilantro). Process until combined. Serve with hot and cold cuts of meat, or seafood such as prawns (shrimp), fish and scallops. Makes 375 ml (13 fl oz/$1^1/_2$ cups).

HONEY MUSTARD

Combine 235 g ($8^1/_2$ oz/$^2/_3$ cup) honey, 4 tablespoons each of yellow mustard and cider vinegar, and 2 tablespoons of olive oil in a small pan. Stir over medium heat for 5 minutes, or until thickened. Allow the mixture to cool completely, then spoon into clean jars. Seal the jars, then label and date them. Honey mustard is delicious served with beef, ham or veal. Makes 175 g (6 oz/$^2/_3$ cup).

Creamy potato gratin

SERVES 6 PREPARATION TIME 20 minutes
COOKING TIME 40 minutes

750 g (1 lb 10 oz) waxy or all-purpose potatoes
1 onion
125 g (4½ oz/1 cup) grated cheddar cheese
375 ml (13 fl oz/1½ cups) cream
2 teaspoons chicken stock (bouillon) powder

Preheat the oven to 180°C (350°F/Gas 4). Thinly slice the potatoes and slice the onion into rings.

Arrange a layer of overlapping potato slices in a baking dish and top with a layer of onion rings. Divide the grated cheese in half and set aside one half for topping. Sprinkle a little of the remaining cheese over the onion. Continue layering in this order until all the potato and the onion have been used, finishing with a little cheese.

Combine the cream with the chicken stock powder and whisk gently until thoroughly combined. Pour the mixture over the potato and onion and sprinkle with the reserved cheese. Bake for 40 minutes, or until the potato is tender, the cheese has melted and the top is golden brown.

Cauliflower cheese

SERVES 4 PREPARATION TIME 15 minutes
COOKING TIME 20 minutes

500 g (1 lb 2 oz) cauliflower
2 tablespoons fresh breadcrumbs
3 tablespoons grated cheddar cheese

CHEESE SAUCE
30 g (1 oz) butter
3 tablespoons plain (all-purpose) flour
315 ml (10¾ fl oz/1¼ cups) warm milk
1 teaspoon dijon mustard
60 g (2¼ oz/½ cup) grated cheddar cheese
50 g (1¾ oz/½ cup) freshly grated parmesan cheese

Lightly grease a 1.5 litre (52 fl oz/6 cup) heatproof dish. Cut the cauliflower into small pieces and cook in a pan of lightly salted boiling water for 10 minutes, or until just tender. Drain thoroughly, transfer to the prepared dish and keep warm.

To make the cheese sauce, melt the butter in a pan over low heat. Stir in the flour and cook for 1 minute, or until pale and foaming. Remove from the heat and gradually stir in the milk and mustard. Return to the heat and stir constantly until the sauce boils and thickens. Reduce the heat and simmer for 2 minutes, then remove from the heat. Add the cheddar and parmesan and stir until just melted. Season the sauce with salt and white pepper, to taste. Pour over the cauliflower.

Combine the breadcrumbs and cheddar and sprinkle over the sauce. Grill (broil) under medium heat until the top is brown and bubbling. Serve immediately.

Green mango chutney

MAKES 750 ml (26 fl oz/3 cups) PREPARATION TIME 20 minutes COOKING TIME 55 minutes

6 medium (2.6 kg/5 lb 12 oz) firm green mangoes
1 large onion, finely chopped
170 ml (5½ fl oz/⅔ cup) white vinegar
95 g (3¼ oz/½ cup firmly packed) light brown sugar
165 g (5¾ oz/¾ cup) sugar
2 teaspoons ground ginger
2 teaspoons garam marsala

Remove the skin from the mangoes and chop the flesh into 1 cm (½ inch) pieces. Place the mango in a large pan with the remaining ingredients and 1 teaspoon of salt. Stir over medium heat, without boiling, for 5 minutes, until the sugar has dissolved.

Bring to the boil, then reduce the heat and simmer for about 45 minutes, until the mixture is very thick and pulpy. Stir often during cooking to prevent the chutney from sticking and burning on the bottom, especially toward the end of the cooking time.

Spoon immediately into clean, warm jars and seal. Turn the jars upside down for 2 minutes, then invert and cool. Label and date. Leave for 1 month before opening to allow the flavours to develop. Store in a cool, dark place for up to 12 months. Refrigerate the chutney after opening for up to 6 weeks.

NOTE: Choose firm, green mangoes that have no bruises or blemishes.

Minted peas

SERVES 6 PREPARATION TIME 5 minutes
COOKING TIME 6 minutes

620 g (1 lb 6 oz/4 cups) fresh or frozen peas
4 sprigs mint
30 g (1 oz) butter
2 tablespoons shredded mint

Put the peas in a saucepan and pour in water to just cover the peas. Add the mint sprigs.

Bring to the boil and simmer for 5 minutes (only 2 minutes if frozen), or until the peas are just tender. Drain and discard the mint sprigs. Return to the saucepan and add the butter and shredded mint. Stir over low heat until the butter has melted. Season with salt and cracked pepper.

Beans with garlic butter crumbs and hazelnuts

SERVES 6 PREPARATION TIME 10 minutes
COOKING TIME 10 minutes

15 g (½ oz) unsalted butter
1 garlic clove, crushed
40 g (1½ oz/½ cup) fresh ciabatta breadcrumbs
finely grated zest of ¼ lemon
1 tablespoon finely chopped flat-leaf (Italian) parsley
3 tablespoons hazelnuts, skinned, lightly toasted and chopped
500 g (1 lb 2 oz) green beans, trimmed

Melt the butter in a frying pan, add the garlic and cook over low heat for 1 minute without browning. Increase the heat to medium–high, stir in the breadcrumbs and lemon zest and toss until the breadcrumbs are lightly browned. Add the parsley and hazelnuts and season with sea salt and freshly ground black pepper.

Meanwhile, bring a saucepan of salted water to the boil, add the beans and cook for 4 minutes, or until tender. Drain well.

Place the beans on a serving dish and pile the garlic butter crumbs on top. Serve at once.

Brussels sprouts in mustard butter

SERVES 4 PREPARATION TIME 15 minutes
COOKING TIME 20 minutes

500 g (1 lb 2 oz) brussels sprouts
30 g (1 oz) butter
3 teaspoons wholegrain mustard
2 teaspoons honey

Trim the ends and remove any loose leaves from the brussels sprouts. Make a small slit across the base of each stem. Put the brussels sprouts in a large steamer and cover with a lid. Sit the steamer over a saucepan of boiling water and steam for 15 minutes, or until tender. Refresh under cold water to stop the cooking process.

Put the butter, mustard and honey in a saucepan over low heat and stir to melt the butter. Add the sprouts and toss until well coated in the butter mixture and heated through. Pile onto a plate and serve immediately.

Asparagus with butter and parmesan

SERVES 4–6 PREPARATION TIME 15 minutes
COOKING TIME 3 minutes

300 g (10½ oz) asparagus
40 g (1½ oz) butter, melted
parmesan cheese shavings, to serve

Snap any thick woody ends from the asparagus and discard. Peel the bottom half of each spear with a vegetable peeler if the skin is very thick.

Plunge the asparagus into a saucepan of boiling water and cook for 2–3 minutes, or until the asparagus is bright green and just tender. Drain and place on serving plates. Drizzle with a little melted butter. Top with parmesan shavings and sprinkle with cracked black pepper.

NOTE: You can use green, purple or white asparagus for this recipe, or a combination. Lightly toasted, crushed hazelnuts or pecan nuts can be sprinkled over the top.

'Blessed is the season which engages the whole world in a conspiracy of love.'

HAMILTON WRIGHT MABIE

Rice salad

SERVES 6–8 PREPARATION TIME 30 minutes plus 1 hour refrigeration COOKING TIME 20 minutes

- 300 g (10½ oz/1½ cups) long-grain rice
- 80 g (2¾ oz/½ cup) fresh or frozen peas
- 3 spring onions (scallions), sliced
- 1 green capsicum (pepper), finely diced
- 1 red capsicum (pepper), finely diced
- 310 g (11 oz) tinned corn kernels, drained, rinsed
- 3 tablespoons chopped mint

DRESSING

- 125 ml (4 fl oz/½ cup) extra virgin olive oil
- 2 tablespoons lemon juice
- 1 garlic clove, crushed
- 1 teaspoon sugar

Bring a large saucepan of water to the boil and stir in the rice. Return to the boil and cook for 12–15 minutes, or until tender. Drain and cool.

Cook the peas in a small saucepan of boiling water for about 2 minutes. Rinse under cold water and drain well.

For the dressing, whisk together the oil, juice, garlic and sugar in a small jug, then season.

Combine the rice, peas, spring onion, capsicum, corn and mint in a large bowl. Add the dressing and mix well. Cover and refrigerate for 1 hour. Transfer to a serving dish.

Coleslaw

SERVES 10 PREPARATION TIME 20 minutes
COOKING TIME nil

- ½ green (savoy) cabbage
- ¼ red cabbage
- 3 carrots, coarsely grated
- 6 radishes, coarsely grated
- 1 capsicum (red pepper), chopped
- 4 spring onions (scallions), sliced
- 3 tablespoons chopped flat-leaf (Italian) parsley
- 250 g (9 oz/1 cup) good-quality mayonnaise

Remove the hard cores from the cabbages and thinly shred the leaves with a sharp knife. Place in a large bowl and add the carrot, radish, capsicum, spring onion and parsley.

Add the mayonnaise, season with salt and freshly ground black pepper and toss well.

NOTE: The vegetables can be chopped and refrigerated for up to 3 hours before serving. Combine with the mayonnaise just before serving.

Cold potato salad

SERVES 8 PREPARATION TIME 30 minutes
COOKING TIME 10 minutes

- 1.2 kg (2 lb 10 oz) waxy white or red potatoes, unpeeled and cut into bite-sized pieces
- 2 onions, finely chopped
- 2 green capsicums (peppers), chopped
- 4–5 celery sticks, chopped
- 1 handful finely chopped parsley

DRESSING

- 375 g (13 oz/1½ cups) whole-egg mayonnaise
- 3–4 tablespoons white wine vinegar or lemon juice
- 90 g (3¼ oz/⅓ cup) sour cream

Steam or boil the potatoes for 5–10 minutes, or until just tender (pierce with the point of a small sharp knife—if the potato comes away easily it is ready). Don't let the skins break away. Drain and cool completely.

Combine the onion, green capsicum, celery and parsley with the cooled potato in a large bowl. Reserve some of the parsley for garnishing.

For the dressing, mix together all the ingredients in a bowl and season with salt and black pepper. Pour over the salad and toss gently. Garnish with the reserved parsley.

NOTE: If you accidentally overcook the potatoes, drain them carefully and spread out on a large flat dish or tray and cool completely. Most of the potatoes will firm up if you do this. In this case, you should also take a little extra care when stirring in the mayonnaise.

Hot potato salad

SERVES 8 PREPARATION TIME 15 minutes
COOKING TIME 25 minutes

- 4 bacon slices
- 1.5 kg (3 lb 5 oz) small waxy red potatoes, unpeeled
- 4 spring onions (scallions), sliced
- 3 tablespoons chopped flat-leaf (Italian) parsley

DRESSING

- 170 ml (5½ fl oz/⅔ cup) extra virgin olive oil
- 1 tablespoon dijon mustard
- 80 ml (2½ fl oz/⅓ cup) white wine vinegar

Trim the rind and any excess fat from the bacon, then cook under a hot grill (broiler) until crisp. Chop into small pieces.

Steam or boil the potatoes for 10–15 minutes, or until just tender (pierce with the point of a small sharp knife—if the potato comes away easily it is ready). Don't let the skins break away. Drain and cool slightly.

For the dressing, whisk all the ingredients together in a jug.

Cut the potatoes into quarters and place in a bowl with half the bacon, the spring onion, parsley and some salt and freshly ground black pepper. Pour in half the dressing and toss to coat the potatoes thoroughly. Transfer to a serving bowl, drizzle with the remaining dressing and sprinkle the remaining bacon over the top.

NOTE: This recipe can also be made with diced potatoes if you prefer. The cooking time will depend on the size of the potato pieces.

CHRISTMAS TREE PICTURE

Celebrate the festive season with this sparkling embroidery design, combining the rich colours of traditional Christmas decor with the sheen of metallic beads and buttons.

For a basic counted-thread cross-stitch pattern such as this, be sure to start your stitching at the centre of the chart and the centre of the fabric. When the embroidery is complete, display your work in a frame, as pictured, use it to cover a book or box, or turn it into a wall-hanging.

MATERIALS

- 45 x 40 cm (17¾ x 16 inch) piece of 28-count evenweave linen in natural
- 1 skein DMC stranded embroidery cotton, ecru
- 1 skein DMC stranded embroidery cotton, 3782 (beige)
- 1 skein DMC stranded embroidery cotton, 500 (dark green)
- 1 skein DMC stranded embroidery cotton, 3371 (dark brown)
- 1 skein DMC stranded embroidery cotton, 3799 (dark grey)
- Mill Hill seed beads in colours 03021 (cream), 03039 (copper), 03037 (mixed metallics), 02021 (pewter grey)
- About 30 extra glass beads approximately 7 mm (¼ inch) diameter in warm natural colours
- Machine sewing thread to match design
- 30 cm (12 inches) of 6 mm (¼ inch) silk ribbon to tie gifts

TOOLS

- Tapestry needle No 24
- Beading needle

1 The Christmas tree design is worked in cross stitch over two threads in three strands of the stranded cotton (the graphs are on pages 214 and 215).

2 Mark the vertical centre of the fabric with a line of long running stitches in a contrasting thread.

3 Start cross stitching the design at the star in the centre of the fabric, 8 cm (3¼ inch) down from the top edge.

4 Work the star, tree and gifts according to the graphs and thread guides. Match the centre lines and the top and bottom of the two charts.

5 Next, scatter the small Mill Hill beads and the larger beads over the surface of the tree, arranging them in a pleasing design, and stitch into place with a single strand of light-coloured machine sewing thread and a beading needle.

6 Lastly, thread the silk ribbon onto the tapestry needle and tie it around the gifts below the tree.

THE CHRISTMAS TREE

Of all Christmas traditions, having a tree in the home is probably the most universally accepted. Decorating the tree began in the sixteenth century at the time of Martin Luther. He took a fir tree home and put candles on it to symbolise the starry night in Bethlehem when Christ was born. In 1776, German soldiers who were taking part in the American War of Independence brought the custom to America. Britain had to wait until 1840 when the German-born Prince Albert, who married Queen Victoria, set up a tree for their children at Windsor Castle and popularised the idea. The custom slowly spread.

Waldorf salad

SERVES 4–6 PREPARATION TIME 20 minutes
COOKING TIME nil

2 green apples, cut into small pieces
2 red apples, cut into small pieces
2 tablespoons lemon juice
4 celery sticks, sliced
3 tablespoons walnut pieces
250 g (9 oz/1 cup) whole-egg mayonnaise
chopped flat-leaf (Italian) parsley, to garnish (optional)

Put the apple in a large bowl, drizzle with the lemon juice and toss to coat (this prevents the apples from discolouring). Mix in the celery and most of the walnut pieces.

Add the mayonnaise to the bowl and toss until well coated. Season to taste. Spoon the salad into a serving bowl, sprinkle with the remaining walnut pieces and serve, garnished with the parsley.

Caesar salad

SERVES 6 PREPARATION TIME 25 minutes
COOKING TIME 20 minutes

1 small baguette
2 tablespoons olive oil
2 garlic cloves, halved
4 bacon slices (trimmed of fat)
2 cos (romaine) lettuces
10 anchovy fillets, halved lengthways
100 g (3½ oz/1 cup) shaved parmesan cheese
parmesan cheese shavings, extra, to serve

DRESSING
1 egg yolk
2 garlic cloves, crushed
2 teaspoons dijon mustard
2 anchovy fillets
2 tablespoons white wine vinegar
1 tablespoon worcestershire sauce
185 ml (6 fl oz/¾ cup) olive oil

Preheat the oven to 180°C (350°F/Gas 4). Cut the baguette into 15 thin slices and brush both sides of each slice with oil. Spread them on a baking tray and bake for 10–15 minutes, or until golden brown. Leave to cool slightly, then rub each side of each slice with the cut edge of a garlic clove. The croutons can then be broken into pieces or cut into small cubes.

Cook the bacon under a hot grill (broiler) until crisp. Drain on paper towels until cooled, then break into chunky pieces.

Tear the lettuce into pieces and put in a large serving bowl with the bacon, anchovies, croutons and parmesan.

To make the dressing, place the egg yolks, garlic, mustard, anchovies, wine vinegar and worcestershire sauce in a food processor or blender. Season and process for 20 seconds, or until smooth. With the motor running, add enough oil in ½a thin stream to make the dressing thick and creamy.

Drizzle the dressing over the salad and toss very gently until well distributed. Sprinkle the parmesan shavings over the top.

Desserts

Steamed pudding

- SERVES 10–12
- PREPARATION TIME 40 minutes plus overnight soaking
- COOKING TIME 8 hours

640 g (1 lb 7 oz/4 cups) mixed sultanas (golden raisins), currants and raisins
330 g (11½ oz/1⅔ cups) mixed dried fruit, chopped
3 tablespoons mixed peel (mixed candied citrus peel)
125 ml (4 fl oz/½ cup) brown ale
2 tablespoons rum or brandy
80 ml (2½ fl oz/⅓ cup) orange juice
80 ml (2½ fl oz/⅓ cup) lemon juice
1 teaspoon finely grated orange zest
1 teaspoon finely grated lemon zest
225 g (8 oz) suet, grated
245 g (8½ oz/1⅓ cups) soft brown sugar
3 eggs, lightly beaten
200 g (7 oz/2½ cups) fresh white breadcrumbs
90 g (3¼ oz/¾ cup) self-raising flour
1 teaspoon mixed (pumpkin pie) spice
¼ teaspoon grated nutmeg
100 g (3½ oz/⅔ cup) blanched almonds, roughly chopped

Put the sultanas, currants, raisins, mixed dried fruit, mixed peel, brown ale, rum, orange and lemon juices and zests into a large bowl and stir together. Cover and leave overnight.

Add the suet, brown sugar, eggs, breadcrumbs, flour, spices, almonds and a pinch of salt to the bowl and mix well. The mixture should fall from the spoon—if it is too stiff, add a little more ale.

Put a 2 litre (70 fl oz/8 cup) pudding basin (steamed pudding mould) on a trivet or upturned saucer in a large saucepan with a lid, and pour in enough water to come halfway up the side of the basin. Remove the basin and put the water on to boil. Fill the pudding basin with the pudding mixture.

To cover the pudding, place a sheet of foil on the bench, top with a piece of baking paper and then brush the paper with melted butter. Fold a pleat across the centre of the foil and paper. Put the paper and foil, foil side up, over the basin. Tie a double length of string firmly around the rim of the basin, then tie a double length of string onto that string to form a handle to lower the pudding into the water. If you have a basin with a lid, clip it on at this stage. The paper/foil lid prevents any moisture from getting into the pudding and making it soggy.

Using the handle, carefully lower the pudding into the saucepan and reduce the heat until the water is simmering quickly. Cover the saucepan. Steam the pudding for 8 hours, replenishing it with boiling water when necessary. If you want to keep your pudding and reheat it later, then steam it for 6 hours and steam it for another 2 hours on the day you would like to eat it. Store the pudding in a cool, dry place for up to 3 months.

NOTE: Buy suet from your butcher.

Boiled pudding

SERVES 10–12 PREPARATION TIME 40 minutes plus overnight soaking COOKING TIME 5 hours

- 310 g (11 oz/1⅔ cups) mixed dried fruit
- 3 tablespoons mixed peel (mixed candied citrus peel)
- 640 g (1 lb 7 oz/4 cups) mixed sultanas (golden raisins), currants and raisins
- 125 ml (4 fl oz/½ cup) brown ale
- 2 tablespoons rum or brandy
- 2 tablespoons orange juice
- 2 tablespoons lemon juice
- 1 tablespoon grated orange zest
- 1 tablespoon grated lemon zest
- 225 g (8 oz) suet, grated
- 245 g (9 oz/1⅓ cups) soft brown sugar
- 3 eggs, lightly beaten
- 200 g (7 oz/2½ cups) white breadcrumbs
- 90 g (3¼ oz/¾ cup) self-raising flour
- 1 teaspoon mixed (pumpkin pie) spice
- ¼ teaspoon freshly grated nutmeg
- 100 g (3½ oz/⅔ cup) blanched almonds, chopped
- plain (all-purpose) flour, extra, for dusting

Finely chop the mixed dried fruit and put in a bowl with the mixed peel, sultanas, currants, raisins, ale, rum, orange and lemon juice and zest. Cover and leave overnight. Mix the fruit with the remaining ingredients and a pinch of salt. Leave for 10 minutes.

Half fill a large saucepan with water, cover and bring to the boil. Cut an 80 cm (32 inch) square from a piece of calico. Add the calico to the saucepan and simmer for 20 minutes. Wearing rubber gloves and using tongs, remove the calico from the boiling water and wring out well. Cover the pan and keep at a constant simmer.

Spread out the calico on a work surface. Cover with about 60 g (2¼ oz/½ cup) of flour, leaving a border. Spread the flour with your hands to get an even covering (this forms a seal between the pudding and the water). You will need to cover enough of the calico with flour so that when the cloth is gathered up the pudding mixture is completedly enclosed by the floured calico.

Spoon the pudding mixture into the centre of the cloth. Bring the points of the cloth together over the top and gather in the material. Leaving room at the top for expansion, tie the top with string. Tie another length of string around the top, long enough to tie to the handles on either side of the saucepan to suspend the pudding (if your saucepan doesn't have suitable handles, suspend a wooden spoon across the saucepan and tie the string to that). Lower the pudding into the simmering water. The pudding should float, without touching the bottom or side of the pan. Cover, place a few tins of fruit on the lid, and boil the pudding for 5 hours. Replenish with boiling water when necessary.

Remove the cooked pudding from the water and hang. Hook up the calico ends to help them dry, and leave the pudding hanging overnight to dry. Untie the calico and spread it out to make sure it dries. When it is dry, rewrap and tie it with string. The pudding will store, hanging in a cool, dry place for up to 4 months. To serve, boil the pudding for 2 hours, hang for 15 minutes, then remove from the cloth.

NOTE: Buy suet from your butcher.

Ice cream pudding

SERVES 10 PREPARATION TIME 1 hour plus freezing
COOKING TIME nil

- 50 g ($1\frac{3}{4}$ oz/$\frac{1}{3}$ cup) toasted almonds, chopped
- 3 tablespoons mixed peel (mixed candied citrus peel)
- 80 g ($2\frac{3}{4}$ oz/$\frac{1}{2}$ cup) raisins, chopped
- 80 g ($2\frac{3}{4}$ oz/$\frac{1}{2}$ cup) sultanas (golden raisins)
- 50 g ($1\frac{3}{4}$ oz/$\frac{1}{3}$ cup) currants
- 80 ml ($2\frac{1}{2}$ fl oz/$\frac{1}{3}$ cup) rum
- 1 litre (35 fl oz/4 cups) good-quality vanilla ice cream
- 105 g ($3\frac{1}{2}$ oz/$\frac{1}{2}$ cup) red and green glacé (candied) cherries, quartered
- 1 teaspoon mixed (pumpkin pie) spice
- 1 teaspoon ground cinnamon
- $\frac{1}{2}$ teaspoon freshly grated nutmeg
- 1 litre (35 fl oz/4 cups) chocolate ice cream

Mix the almonds, peel, raisins, sultanas, currants and rum in a bowl, cover with plastic wrap and leave overnight. Chill a 2 litre (70 fl oz/8 cup) pudding basin (steamed pudding mould) in the freezer overnight.

Soften the vanilla ice cream slightly and mix in the glacé cherries. Working quickly, press the ice cream all around the inside of the chilled pudding basin, spreading it evenly to cover the base and side of the basin. Return the basin to the freezer overnight. Check the ice cream a couple of times and spread it evenly to the top.

The next day, mix the spices and chocolate ice cream with the fruit mixture. Spoon it into the centre of the pudding bowl and smooth the top. Freeze overnight, or until very firm. Turn out the pudding onto a chilled plate. Cut into wedges, to serve.

Sago plum pudding with rum butter

SERVES 6–8
PREPARATION TIME 35 minutes plus overnight refrigeration
COOKING TIME 4 HOURS

65 g (2¼ oz/⅓ cup) sago
250 ml (9 fl oz/1 cup) milk
1 teaspoon bicarbonate of soda (baking soda)
140 g (5 oz/¾ cup) dark brown sugar
160 g (5¾ oz/2 cups) fresh white breadcrumbs
80 g (2¾ oz/½ cup) sultanas (golden raisins)
75 g (2½ oz/½ cup) currants
80 g (2¾ oz/½ cup) dried dates, chopped
2 eggs, lightly beaten
60 g (2¼ oz) unsalted butter, melted and cooled
raspberries, to decorate
blueberries, to decorate
icing (confectioners') sugar, to decorate

RUM BUTTER
125 g (4½ oz) butter, softened
140 g (5 oz/¾ cup) dark brown sugar
80 ml (2½ fl oz/⅓ cup) rum

Combine the sago and milk in a bowl, cover and refrigerate overnight.

Lightly grease a 1.5 litre (52 fl oz/6 cup) pudding basin (steamed pudding mould) with butter and line the base with baking paper. Place the empty basin in a large saucepan on a trivet or upturned saucer and pour in enough cold water to come halfway up the side of the basin. Remove the basin and put the water on to boil.

Transfer the soaked sago and milk to a large bowl and stir in the bicarbonate of soda until dissolved. Stir in the sugar, breadcrumbs, dried fruit, beaten eggs and melted butter and mix well. Spoon into the basin and smooth the surface with wet hands. Cover the pudding with baking paper and foil (see page 150).

Cover the basin with the lid and make a string handle. Gently lower the basin into the boiling water, reduce to a fast simmer and cover the saucepan with a tight-fitting lid. Cook for 3½–4 hours, or until a skewer inserted into the centre of the pudding comes out clean. Check the water level every hour and top up the pan with boiling water as necessary.

Carefully remove the pudding basin from the saucepan, remove the coverings and leave for 5 minutes before turning out onto a large serving plate. Loosen the edges with a palette knife, if necessary. Serve decorated with raspberries and blueberries and lightly dusted with icing sugar. Serve hot with cold rum butter.

To make the rum butter, beat the butter and sugar with electric beaters for about 3–4 minutes, or until light and creamy. Gradually beat in the rum, 1 tablespoon at a time. You can add more rum, to taste. Transfer to a serving dish, cover and refrigerate until required.

NOTE: Sago is the starch extracted from the sago palm. It is dried and formed into balls by pushing through a sieve. It is often called pearl sago and is available from supermarkets or health food stores. It is white when uncooked but turns transparent when cooked.

BEADED CHRISTMAS DECORATIONS

Welcome the festive season by adorning rooms and the branches of evergreen trees with sparkling decorations. These decorations could be modified and used as gift-wrapping decorations and even festive earrings, if you wish.

MATERIALS (FOR EACH DECORATION)

- Memory wire in large bangle shape
- 31 silver head pins, 20 mm (¾ inch) long
- 2 silver eye pins, 20 mm (¾ inch) long
- 20 cm (8 inches) of small belcher chain with 3 mm (⅛ inch) links
- 82 silver seed beads, 3 mm (⅛ inch) diameter
- 46 white plastic pearls, 4 mm (3⁄16 inch) diameter
- 1 Swarovski crystal drop with side holes, 18 mm (1 1⁄16 inch) long

TOOLS

- Side cutters
- Round-nose pliers
- Snipe-nose pliers
- Safety glasses

1 Cut the memory wire into a 22 cm (8¾ inch) length using side cutters and create a loop at one end by bending it around the round-nose pliers. Use the side cutters to cut the belcher chain into one length of 29 chain links and one length of 35 chain links.

2 Thread beads onto the head pins: thread 15 pins with two seed beads on each and 16 pins with a single pearl on each. Cut the head pins with side cutters, leaving 10 mm (⅜ inch), and then create a loop by bending the pin around the round-nose pliers.

3 Thread the beads and chain onto the memory wire in the following sequence: two seed beads, one pearl, two seed beads, one pearl, two seed beads, one end of a 55 mm (2 3⁄16 inch) length of belcher chain, three seed beads, one pearl, three seed beads, one end of a 68 mm (21 1⁄16 inch) chain. Next thread on two seed beads and one pearl and repeat this process 13 times.

4 Now thread on two seed beads, then the loose end of the 68 mm (21 1⁄16 inch) length of belcher chain. Repeat the same combination of beads and chain as on the opposite side of the decoration, but in reverse order to make sure the beading is symmetrical. To complete the circular form and make sure the beads sit tightly together, cut off the excess memory wire, leaving 10 mm (⅜ inch), and loop the cut end into an eyelet using the round-nose pliers.

5 Attach the beaded head pins to the chains. Use seven pearl and seven seed bead drops for the top chain and nine pearl and eight seed bead drops for the bottom chain. Attach the first post to the first loose chain link, making sure the bead is hanging straight. Repeat this process using every second link of chain.

6 Cut 32 mm (1¼ inch) of belcher chain (15 links) and attach either end of this length of chain to each rounded end of the memory wire using snipe-nose pliers (see Basic techniques, page 19). Using the same technique, attach an eye pin to the middle link of the chain. Bend the post of the eye pin around the base of the round-nose pliers to create a large hook to hang the decoration.

7 Thread the crystal onto an eye pin and create a loop at the post end, making sure this loop is flat. Open the loops with snipe-nose pliers and hook them into the loops on the ends of the memory wire.

STEP 3 Begin threading beads, pearls and chain onto the wire.

STEP 4 Continue the pattern of beading to create a symmetrical arrangement.

STEP 5 Attach the beaded head pins to the chains.

STEP 5 Alternate beads and pearls across the chain links.

Choc-ginger puddings

MAKES 10
PREPARATION TIME 45 minutes plus overnight soaking
COOKING TIME 1 hour 15 minutes

320 g (11¼ oz/2 cups) raisins, chopped
200 g (7 oz/1⅓ cups) currants
110 g (3¾ oz/⅔ cup) pitted dates, chopped
75 g (2½ oz/⅓ cup) glacé (candied) ginger, chopped
160 g (5¾ oz/1 cup) sultanas (golden raisins)
100 g (3½ oz) dried pears, chopped
100 g (3½ oz) dried apricots, chopped
175 g (6 oz/1 cup) dark chocolate bits
75 g (2½ oz/½ cup) pistachios, chopped
125 ml (4 fl oz/½ cup) brandy
250 g (9 oz) unsalted butter, frozen and grated
185 g (6½ oz/1 cup) dark brown sugar
1 tablespoon treacle or molasses
80 ml (2¾ fl oz/⅓ cup) orange juice
80 ml (2¾ fl oz/⅓ cup) lemon juice
1 teaspoon finely grated orange zest
1 teaspoon finely grated lemon zest
4 eggs, lightly beaten
1 teaspoon bicarbonate of soda (baking soda)
185 g (6½ oz/1½ cups) plain (all-purpose) flour
60 g (2¼ oz/½ cup) self-raising flour
2 teaspoons mixed (pumpkin pie) spice
2 teaspoons ground cinnamon
1 teaspoon freshly grated nutmeg
80 g (2¾ oz/1 cup) fresh breadcrumbs
plain (all-purpose) flour, extra, for dusting

Put all the fruit, chocolate and pistachios into a large basin and stir in the brandy. Cover with plastic wrap and leave overnight.

Bring two large saucepans of water to the boil. Cut ten 30 cm (12 inch) squares from a sheet of calico. Put the calico in one of the saucepans of boiling water for 15 minutes, then remove with tongs and, with gloved hands, wring out the water.

Put the butter in a large bowl and stir in the sugar, treacle, juices and zests and the eggs. Add the combined sifted bicarbonate of soda, flours and spices in two batches. Stir in the fruit and breadcrumbs.

Place a calico square on a flat surface and rub liberally with flour, leaving a border of calico. Place a loosely packed cup of the pudding mixture into the centre of the cloth. Gather and tie the cloth into a neat ball, pleating the calico. Tie firmly with string around the top and tie the end of the string to enable the puddings to hang from a wooden spoon. Repeat with all the pudding mixture and calico. Place half the puddings in each saucepan of boiling water, then sit the lids over the spoons to keep most of the steam in. Simmer for 1 hour.

Hang the puddings overnight in a cool place to dry, then refrigerate in an airtight container. Keep for up to 1 month.

To reheat, lower the puddings into a pan of boiling water and boil for 30 minutes. Remove the cloths and serve individually, with cream or custard.

Fig pudding

SERVES 8 PREPARATION TIME 40 minutes
COOKING TIME 3 hours 40 minutes

- 500 g (1 lb 2 oz) dried figs, chopped
- 440 ml (15¼ fl oz/1¾ cups) milk
- 240 g (8½ oz/3 cups) coarse fresh breadcrumbs
- 140 g (5 oz/¾ cup) soft brown sugar
- 250 g (9 oz/2 cups) self-raising flour, sifted
- 2 eggs, lightly beaten
- 150 g (5½ oz) unsalted butter, melted and cooled

Grease a 2 litre (70 fl oz/8 cup) pudding basin (steamed pudding mould) with butter and line the base with baking paper. Place the empty basin in a saucepan on a trivet or upturned saucer. Pour in enough water to come halfway up the side of the basin. Remove the basin and put the water on to boil.

Put the figs in a saucepan with the milk. Bring to a simmer, cover and cook over low heat for 10 minutes. Stir to combine. Combine the breadcrumbs, sugar and flour in a bowl. Stir in the soaked figs and any liquid, the eggs and butter. Spoon into the basin. Cover the pudding with baking paper and foil (see page 150). Cover the basin with a lid and make a handle with string.

Lower the pudding basin into the boiling water, reduce to a fast simmer and cover the saucepan with a tight-fitting lid. Cook for 3½ hours, checking the water every hour and topping up with boiling water as necessary. The pudding is cooked when a skewer inserted in the centre comes out clean. Leave for 5 minutes before turning out. Serve with custard or cream.

Sauces

CRÈME ANGLAISE

Whisk 3 egg yolks and 2 tablespoons caster (superfine) sugar together in a heatproof bowl for 2 minutes, or until light and creamy. Heat 375 ml (13 fl oz/1½ cups) of milk until almost boiling, then pour onto the sugar mixture, whisky constantly. Return the custard to the clean pan and stir for 5 minutes, or until thickened enough to coat the back of a spoon. Don't allow the mixture to boil or it will curdle. Remove from the heat, stir in ½ teaspoon natural vanilla extract and serve immediately. Makes 500 ml (17 fl oz/2 cups).

VANILLA CUSTARD

Combine 250 ml (9 fl oz/1 cup) milk and 3 tablespoons cream in a pan. Bring to the boil, then remove from the heat immediately. In a heatproof bowl, whisk 3 egg yolks, 125 g (4½ oz/½ cup) caster (superfine) sugar and 2 teaspoons cornflour (cornstarch). Slowly pour the hot milk and cream into the egg mixture, whisking continuously. Return to the pan and stir over low heat for 5 minutes, or until thickened. Do not allow the custard to boil. Remove from the heat and stir in ½ teaspoon natural vanilla extract. Serve immediately. Makes 500 ml (17 fl oz/2 cups).

ZABAGLIONE

Put 8 egg yolks and 90 g (3¼ oz/⅓ cup) caster (superfine) sugar in a heatproof bowl and beat with electric beaters until thick and pale. Put the bowl over a simmering pan of water and beat continuously, gradually adding 315 ml (10¾ fl oz/1¼ cups) of Marsala. Beat for 5 minutes, or until thick and frothy. The custard is ready when you can draw a line through the mixture with a spoon and it leaves a trail. Makes 500 ml (17 fl oz/2 cups).

BRANDY BUTTER

Using electric beaters, beat 250 g (9 oz) softened unsalted butter and 185 g (6½ oz/1½ cups) sifted icing (confectioners') sugar until smooth and creamy. Gradually add 3 tablespoons brandy, beating thoroughly. Refrigerate until required. Makes about 250 ml (9 fl oz/1 cup).

BRANDY CREAM SAUCE

Beat 2 egg yolks and 90 g (3¼ oz/⅓ cup) caster (superfine) sugar until thick and pale and the sugar has dissolved. Stir in 80 ml (2½ fl oz/⅓ cup) brandy and fold in 250 ml (9 fl oz/1 cup) cream. Beat 2 egg whites in a clean, dry bowl until soft peaks form. Fold into the sauce and serve immediately. Makes 375 ml (13 fl oz/1½ cups).

WHISKY SAUCE

Melt 2 tablespoons of butter in a pan over low heat. Remove from the heat, add 40 g (1½ oz/⅓ cup) of plain (all-purpose) flour and stir to combine. Gradually whisk in 500 ml (17 fl oz/2 cups) of milk and 2 tablespoons caster (superfine) sugar. Return the pan to medium heat and whisk until the mixture boils and thickens. Reduce the heat and simmer, stirring occasionally, for 10 minutes. Remove from the heat and stir in 80 ml (2½ fl oz/⅓ cup) whisky, 2 teaspoons butter and 1 tablespoon thick (double/heavy) cream. Cover with plastic wrap until ready to serve. Makes 500 ml (17 fl oz/2 cups).

Treacle tart

SERVES 4–6 PREPARATION TIME 30 minutes plus chilling
COOKING TIME 35 minutes

PASTRY
150 g (5½ oz/1¼ cups) plain (all-purpose) flour
90 g (3¼ oz) chilled unsalted butter, chopped
2–3 tablespoons iced water

350 g (12 oz/1 cup) golden syrup or dark corn syrup
25 g (1 oz) unsalted butter
½ teaspoon ground ginger
140 g (5 oz/1¾ cups) fresh white breadcrumbs
1 egg, lightly beaten, to glaze
icing (confectioners') sugar, to dust (optional)

To make the pastry, sift the flour into a large bowl. Using your fingertips, rub in the butter until the mixture resembles fine breadcrumbs. Add almost all the iced water and mix to a firm dough, with a flat-bladed knife, using a cutting action. Add more water if the dough is too dry. Turn onto a lightly floured work surface and gather together into a ball. Cover with plastic wrap and refrigerate for 20 minutes.

Grease a 20 cm (8 inch) flan (tart) tin. Roll out the pastry to fit the base and side of the tin, allowing a 4 cm (1½ inch) overhang. Ease the pastry into the tin and trim by running a rolling pin firmly across the top of the tin. Re-roll the pastry trimmings to a rectangle 10 x 20 cm (4 x 8 inches). Using a sharp knife or fluted pastry wheel, cut into long 1 cm (½ inch) strips. Cover the pastry-lined tin and strips with plastic wrap and refrigerate for 20 minutes. Preheat the oven to 180°C (350°F/Gas 4).

Combine the golden syrup, butter and ginger in a small saucepan and stir over low heat until the butter melts. Stir in the breadcrumbs until combined. Pour the mixture into the pastry case and lay half the pastry strips over the tart, starting at the centre and working outwards. Arrange the remaining pastry strips over the tart in a lattice pattern. Brush the lattice with beaten egg. Bake for 30 minutes, or until the pastry is lightly golden. Serve the tart warm or at room temperature. You can dust the top with icing sugar and serve with ice cream or cream.

Berry pie

SERVES 4–6 PREPARATION TIME 30 minutes
COOKING TIME 45 minutes

PASTRY
125 g (4½ oz/1 cup) self-raising flour
125 g (4½ oz/1 cup) plain (all-purpose) flour
125 g (4½ oz) chilled unsalted butter, chopped
2 tablespoons caster (superfine) sugar
1 egg, lightly beaten
3–4 tablespoons milk

2 tablespoons cornflour (cornstarch)
2–4 tablespoons caster (superfine) sugar, to taste
1 teaspoon grated orange zest
1 tablespoon orange juice
600 g (1 lb 5 oz) fresh berries (such as boysenberries, blackberries, loganberries, mulberries, raspberries or youngberries)
1 egg yolk, mixed with 1 teaspoon water, to glaze
icing (confectioners') sugar, to dust

To make the pastry, sift the flours into a large bowl. Using your fingertips, rub in the chopped butter until the mixture resembles fine breadcrumbs. Stir in the sugar, then add the egg and almost all the milk. Mix with a flat-bladed knife, using a cutting action, until the mixture comes together in beads. Add more milk if the dough is too dry. Turn out onto a lightly floured surface and gather into a ball. Divide the pastry into two portions and roll out on a sheet of baking paper, making sure one is the right size to fit the top of a 750 ml (26 fl oz/3 cup) pie dish. Cover with plastic wrap and refrigerate for 30 minutes.

Mix the cornflour, caster sugar, orange zest and juice in a saucepan. Add half the berries to the pan and stir over low heat for 5 minutes, or until the mixture boils and thickens. Remove the pan from the heat and set aside to cool. Add the remaining berries to the pan, carefully pour into the pie dish and smooth the surface with the back of a spoon.

Preheat the oven to 180°C (350°F/Gas 4). Place the pie top over the fruit and trim the edges. Do not stretch the pastry or it may shrink during baking. Using heart-shaped cutters of various sizes, cut out enough hearts from the remaining pastry to cover the top of the pie. Arrange the hearts on top of the pie, moistening with a little water to make them stick.

Brush all over the surface with the egg glaze and bake for 35–40 minutes, until the pastry is crisp and golden brown. Dust with icing sugar just before serving. Serve the berry pie warm or cold.

NOTES: Use just one variety of berry or a combination if you prefer. If you want to make the pie when the berries are out of season, use frozen berries. Defrost the berries thoroughly, reserving the juice. Add the berries and juice to the filling and omit the orange juice. You can use tinned berries if you drain them well first.

Nesselrode

- SERVES 8
- PREPARATION TIME 25 minutes plus freezing
- COOKING TIME nil

5 egg yolks
185 g (6½ oz/¾ cup) caster (superfine) sugar
1 litre (35 fl oz/4 cups) cream
1 teaspoon natural vanilla extract
1 tablespoon brandy
165 g (5¾ oz/½ cup) chestnut purée
75 g (2½ oz/½ cup) currants
80 g (2¾ oz/½ cup) sultanas (golden raisins)
3 tablespoons glacé (candied) cherries, chopped
95 g (3¼ oz/½ cup) mixed peel (mixed candied citrus peel)

TO DECORATE
toasted flaked almonds
selection of glacé (candied) cherries, angelica, crystallised violets or sugared grapes, fresh fruit or sugared rose petals
250 ml (9 fl oz/1 cup) cream, extra, whipped (optional)

Beat the egg yolks and sugar in a small bowl with electric beaters until pale, thick and fluffy. Pour half the cream into a pan and heat until almost boiling. Gradually pour onto the eggs and sugar, mixing well. Strain the mixture back into the clean pan and place over low heat.

Using a wooden spoon, stir constantly around the base and side of the pan until the custard thickens slightly and coats the back of the spoon. Do not boil or the custard will curdle. Remove from the heat and stir in the vanilla and brandy. Add the chestnut purée and beat well to combine. Strain the mixture and allow to cool.

Beat the remaining cream in a bowl until soft peaks form, then fold into the cooled custard mixture.

Put the currants and sultanas in a bowl and cover completely with warm water.

Pour the cream mixture into a shallow metal tray and freeze for 2–3 hours, or until the mixture is just starting to freeze. Transfer to a large bowl or food processor, beat until smooth, then pour back into the tray and return to the freezer. Repeat this step three times. Before the final freezing, stir in the glacé cherries, mixed peel and the well-drained currants and sultanas.

Lightly oil a 2 litre (70 fl oz/8 cup) charlotte mould or cake tin, line the mould with plastic wrap, then pour in the cream mixture. Cover the surface with plastic wrap and freeze for at least 8 hours, or until firm.

Invert the pudding onto a plate and carefully peel away the plastic. Decorate the sides of the pudding with lines of toasted almonds, pieces of angelica, halved glacé cherries, crystallised violets or sugared fruits. The nesselrode can be returned to the freezer after it is decorated. When ready to serve, pile whipped cream over the top, then top that with piped whipped cream.

Cranberry creams

SERVES 6 PREPARATION TIME 20 minutes plus 4 hours chilling COOKING TIME 30 minutes

- 4 egg yolks
- 3 tablespoons caster (superfine) sugar
- 300 ml (10½ fl oz) cream
- 125 ml (4 fl oz/½ cup) milk
- finely grated zest of 1 orange
- icing (confectioners') sugar, to serve

CRANBERRY COMPOTE

- 150 g (5½ oz) fresh or frozen cranberries
- 3 tablespoons caster (superfine) sugar
- juice of 1 orange

Preheat the oven to 150°C (300°F/Gas 2). Place six 170 ml (5½ fl oz/⅔ cup) ceramic pots or decorative cups in a large roasting tin.

To make the cranberry compote, combine the cranberries, sugar and orange juice in a small saucepan. Bring to the boil and stir until the sugar has dissolved. Reduce the heat to low, mash the cranberries with a potato masher and cook for 5 minutes, or until thick. Spoon the cranberry compote evenly over the base of each pot.

Beat the egg yolks and sugar in a bowl using electric beaters until thick and creamy. Combine the cream, milk and orange zest in a saucepan and bring to scalding point. Gradually beat the cream mixture into the egg yolk mixture. Return the mixture to the cleaned saucepan and stir constantly over low heat for 2–3 minutes, or until the mixture has thickened a little and coats the back of the spoon.

Pour the custard over the back of the spoon into the pots, so as not to disturb the fruit. Half fill the roasting tin with boiling water and bake for 20 minutes, or until the custard is just set. Take care not to overcook, the centre should wobble slightly. Set aside to cool, cover with plastic wrap and refrigerate for 4 hours, or overnight.

Serve the cranberry creams dusted with sifted icing sugar.

Ice cream bombe

SERVES 8 PREPARATION TIME 20 minutes plus overnight freezing COOKING TIME 3 minutes

1 large mango, finely chopped
160 g (5½ oz/1 cup) canned pineapple pieces, drained
3 tablespoons Grand Marnier
250 g (9 oz) strawberries, puréed
400 g (14 oz) can sweetened condensed milk
625 ml (21½ fl oz/2½ cups) cream
80 g (2¾ oz) dessert nougat, chopped (see Note)
3 tablespoons roughly chopped unsalted pistachios
strawberries, extra, halved, to garnish

TOFFEE BARK
90 g (3¼ oz/⅓ cup) caster (superfine) sugar

Lightly grease a 2 litre (64 fl oz/8 cup) metal pudding basin (steamed pudding mould) and line with plastic wrap, allowing it to hang over the side of the basin. Put in the freezer until ready to use. Drain the mango and pineapple in a sieve.

Mix the Grand Marnier, strawberry purée and condensed milk in a large bowl. Whisk the cream to soft peaks, then add to the bowl and continue whisking until thick. Fold in the drained fruits, nougat and pistachios. Pour the mixture into the pudding basin, cover with plastic wrap and freeze overnight, or until firm.

To serve, remove the plastic wrap from the base and invert the pudding onto a chilled serving plate. Remove the bowl, but leave the plastic wrap and refrigerate for 15–25 minutes to soften slightly.

For the toffee bark, line a baking tray with baking paper. Heat the sugar over low heat in a heavy-based saucepan for 2–3 minutes, until melted and golden. Carefully pour onto the baking tray. Tilt the tray to get a thin, even layer of toffee and cool slightly. While the toffee is still pliable, drape the paper over a rolling pin and allow to cool for 30–60 seconds before peeling away strips of toffee in large irregular shapes. Cool.

Remove the plastic and decorate the bombe with toffee bark and strawberries.

NOTE: Dessert nougat is a soft nougat available from confectionery shops and some delicatessens.

Chocolate hazelnut torte

SERVES 10 PREPARATION TIME 1 hour plus overnight refrigeration COOKING TIME 1 hour 15 minutes

500 g (1 lb 2 oz) dark chocolate, chopped
6 eggs
2 tablespoons Frangelico
165 g (5½ oz/1½ cups) ground hazelnuts
250 ml (9 fl oz/1 cup) cream, whipped
12 whole hazelnuts, lightly roasted

CHOCOLATE TOPPING
200 g (7 oz) dark chocolate, chopped
185 ml (6 fl oz/¾ cup) cream
1 tablespoon Frangelico

Preheat the oven to 150°C (300°F/Gas 2). Grease a deep 20 cm (8 inch) round cake tin and line with baking paper.

Put the chocolate in a heatproof bowl. Half-fill a saucepan with water and bring to the boil. Remove from the heat and place the bowl over the pan, making sure it is not touching the water. Stir occasionally until the chocolate is melted. Put the eggs in a large heatproof bowl and add the Frangelico. Place the bowl over a saucepan of barely simmering water over low heat, making sure it does not touch the water. Beat with an electric mixer on high speed for 7 minutes, or until the mixture is light and foamy. Remove from the heat. Using a metal spoon, quickly and lightly fold the melted chocolate and ground nuts into the egg mixture until just combined. Fold in the cream and pour the mixture into the tin. Place the tin in a shallow baking dish. Pour in enough hot water to come halfway up the side of the tin.

Bake for 1 hour, or until just set. Remove the tin from the baking dish. Cool to room temperature, cover with plastic wrap and refrigerate overnight.

Cut out a 17 cm (7 inch) circle from heavy cardboard. Invert the chilled cake onto the disc so that the base of the cake becomes the top. Place on a wire rack over a baking tray and remove the baking paper. Allow the cake to return to room temperature before you start to decorate it.

To make the topping, combine the chocolate, cream and Frangelico in a small pan. Heat gently over low heat, stirring, until the chocolate is melted and the mixture is smooth. Pour the topping over the cake, tilting to cover the cake evenly. Gently tap the baking tray on the bench so that the top is level and the icing runs completely down the side of the cake. Place the hazelnuts around the edge of the cake. Refrigerate just until the topping has set and the cake is firm.

Carefully transfer the cake to a serving plate, and cut into thin wedges to serve.

Liqueur fruits

These liqueur-infused fruits are luscious with cream or ice cream, waffles or crepes. They are also great with brioche or panettone spread with ricotta or mascarpone.

PEARS IN MULLED WINE

Put 500 g (1 lb 2 oz/2 cups) sugar and 750 ml (26 fl oz/3 cups) red wine in a large pan. Stir over low heat until the sugar has dissolved. Add 1.25 kg (2 lb 12 oz) peeled, halved and cored small pears, 1 cinnamon stick, 6 cloves, 6 whole allspice and 2 strips each of orange and lemon rind. Cover with a plate to keep the pears submerged. Bring to the boil (at least 90°C), then reduce the heat and simmer for 10 minutes. Arrange the pears in a heatproof, warm, sterilised 1 litre (35 fl oz/4 cup) jar. Boil the syrup for 15 minutes, then mix 125 ml (4 fl oz/½ cup) syrup with 125 ml (4 fl oz/½ cup) brandy and 3 cloves. Pour over the pears to cover, seal and invert for 2 minutes. Store in a cool, dark place for up to a month before using. Refrigerate after opening. Fills a 1 litre (35 fl oz/4 cup) jar.

DRUNKEN PRUNES

Put 750 g (1 lb 10 oz) pitted prunes in a warm, sterilised 1 litre (35 fl oz/4 cup) heatproof jar. Cut a vanilla bean in half lengthways and add to the jar. Add 500 ml (17 fl oz/2 cups) tawny port to cover the prunes, seal and invert for 2 minutes. Leave for at least 1 month before using. Store the prunes for up to 6 months and refrigerate after opening. Fills a 1 litre (35 fl oz/4 cup) jar.

CLEMENTINES OR CUMQUATS IN LIQUEUR

Cut a cross in the tops of 500 g (1 lb 2 oz) clementines or cumquats and pack into warm, sterilised heatproof jars. Put 250 g (9 oz/1 cup) sugar and 185 ml (6 fl oz/¾ cup) water in a saucepan and boil for 1 minute. Stir in 3 tablespoons orange

liqueur, then pour over the fruit. Screw on the lids loosely—do not tighten them. Place layers of cloth on the base of a deep, heavy-based saucepan. Put the jars on top of the cloth and cover with hot water to reach the shoulders of the jars. Bring the water slowly to simmering point, then reduce the heat and simmer for 20 minutes, or until the fruit starts to look clear. Remove the jars. Immediately tighten the lids fully with a tea towel. Cool, label and date. Store in a cool, dark place for 2 months before using, inverting the jars every 2 weeks. Will keep for 6 months. Refrigerate after opening. Fills a 750 ml (26 fl oz/3 cup) jar.

PEACHES IN SPICED SAUTERNES

Cut 4–6 kg (9–13½ lb) ripe freestone peaches in half, discard the stones and pack the peaches into a warm, sterilised 2 litre (70 fl oz/8 cup) heatproof jar with 1 cinnamon stick and 1 star anise. Place 500 g (1 lb 2 oz/2 cups) sugar in a large saucepan, add 500 ml (17 fl oz/2 cups) water and stir over low heat until all the sugar has dissolved. Bring to the boil (at least 90°C) and boil for 5 minutes, then pour the syrup over the peaches and top with 250 ml (9 fl oz/1 cup) of Sauternes. Following the cumquat instructions, simmer in the jar for 10 minutes, or until the syrup reaches 90°C (check with a thermometer). Keep in a cool, dark place for at least 2 weeks before using. Will keep for 6 months. Refrigerate after opening. Fills a 2 litre (70 fl oz/8 cup) jar.

CHERRIES IN VANILLA BRANDY

Prick the skins of 750 g (1 lb 10 oz) cherries with a fine skewer. Heat 375 g (13 oz/1½ cups) sugar with 125 ml (4 fl oz/½ cup) each of brandy and water in a pan, stirring until all the sugar has dissolved. Add the cherries and a vanilla bean and heat until boiling (90°C). Place the cherries and syrup in a warm, sterilised heatproof jar, seal while hot and invert for 2 minutes. Store the cherries in a cool place for 6 weeks, turning every couple of days for the first 2 weeks. Refrigerate after opening. Fills a 1 litre (35 fl oz/4 cup) jar.

Fruit tart

SERVES 6   PREPARATION TIME 40 minutes plus chilling
COOKING TIME 40 minutes

PASTRY
150 g (5½ oz/1¼ cups) plain (all-purpose) flour
2 tablespoons caster (superfine) sugar
90 g (3¼ oz) chilled unsalted butter, chopped
1 egg yolk
1 tablespoon iced water

250 ml (9 fl oz/1 cup) milk
3 egg yolks
3 tablespoons caster (superfine) sugar
2 tablespoons plain (all-purpose) flour
1 teaspoon natural vanilla extract
strawberries, kiwi fruit and blueberries, to decorate
apricot jam (jelly), to glaze

To make the pastry, sift the flour into a bowl. Stir in the sugar and, using your fingertips, rub in the butter until the mixture resembles fine breadcrumbs. Make a well in the centre and add the egg yolk and the iced water. Mix to a dough with a flat-bladed knife, using a cutting action. Turn the pastry out onto a lightly floured work surface and gather together into a ball. Press together gently until smooth, and then roll out to fit a 10 x 34 cm (4 x 13½ inch) loose-based fluted flan (tart) tin. Line the tin with pastry and trim away any excess. Wrap in plastic wrap and refrigerate for 20 minutes. Preheat the oven to 190°C (375°F/Gas 5).

Line the pastry-lined tin with baking paper and spread a layer of baking beads or uncooked rice evenly over the paper. Bake for 15 minutes, then remove the paper and beads and bake for another 20 minutes, or until the pastry is cooked on the base and golden brown around the edge. Cool completely.

Put the milk into a small saucepan and bring to the boil. Set aside while quickly whisking the egg yolks and sugar together in a bowl, until light and creamy. Whisk in the flour. Pour the hot milk slowly onto the egg mixture, whisking constantly. Wash out the pan, return the milk mixture to the pan and bring to the boil over medium heat, stirring with a wire whisk. Boil for 2 minutes, stirring occasionally. Transfer to a bowl, stir in the vanilla, and leave to cool, stirring often to prevent a skin forming. When cooled to room temperature, cover the surface with plastic wrap and refrigerate until cold.

Cut the strawberries in half and peel and slice the kiwi fruit. Spoon the cold custard into the cold pastry shell. Arrange the fruit over the custard, pressing in slightly. Heat the apricot jam in the microwave or a small saucepan until liquid, sieve to remove any lumps, then, using a pastry brush, glaze the fruit with the jam. Serve the tart on the same day. If it is to be left for a while on a hot day, refrigerate it.

NOTE: If you don't have a rectangular tin, this tart may be made in a 23 cm (9 inch) round flan tin. You can use different fruits to top the tart, according to taste and season.

Berries in Champagne jelly

SERVES 8 PREPARATION TIME 10 minutes plus setting time
COOKING TIME 5 minutes

1 litre (35 fl oz/4 cups) Champagne or sparkling white wine
1½ tablespoons powdered gelatine
250 g (9 oz/1 cup) sugar
4 strips lemon rind
4 strips orange rind
250 g (9 oz) small strawberries, hulled
250 g (9 oz) blueberries

Pour half the Champagne or sparkling wine into a bowl and let the bubbles subside. Sprinkle the gelatine over the top in an even layer. Leave until the gelatine is spongy—do not stir. Pour the remaining Champagne into a large saucepan, add the sugar and rinds and heat gently, stirring constantly, until all the sugar has dissolved.

Remove the saucepan from the heat, add the gelatine mixture and stir until thoroughly dissolved. Leave to cool completely, then remove the rind.

Divide the strawberries and blueberries among eight 125 ml (4 fl oz/½ cup) stemmed wine glasses and gently pour the jelly over them. Refrigerate until set. Remove from the refrigerator 15 minutes before serving.

NOTE: If fresh berries aren't in season, use good-quality frozen berries. Thaw the berries on a tray in the refrigerator before using.

Rum and raisin balls

MAKES 45 PREPARATION TIME 30 minutes plus soaking and setting COOKING TIME nil

60 g (2¼ oz/½ cup) raisins
80 ml (2½ fl oz/⅓ cup) dark rum
500 g (1 lb 2 oz) purchased madeira (pound) cake
250 g (9 oz) good-quality marzipan
375 g (13 oz/2½ cups) dark chocolate melts, melted
3 tablespoons slivered almonds, lightly toasted

Line two trays with baking paper.

Combine the raisins and rum in a small bowl and set aside for 1 hour. Strain the rum into a small bowl and set aside. Place the raisins in a separate small bowl.

Trim and discard any dark edges from the cake. Put the cake, marzipan and reserved rum in the bowl of a food processor and process until just combined. Transfer to a bowl and stir in the raisins.

Roll heaped teaspoons of the mixture into balls, place on the baking trays and refrigerate for 1 hour, or until firm. Roll the balls in the chocolate and return to the trays for 30 minutes, or until the chocolate is almost set. Top with the slivered almonds and allow to set.

Pavlova with fresh fruit

SERVES 8 PREPARATION TIME 20 minutes
COOKING TIME 40 minutes

4 egg whites
230 g (8 oz/1 cup) caster (superfine) sugar
375 ml (13 fl oz/1½ cups) cream, whipped
1 banana, sliced
125 g (4½ oz) raspberries
125 g (4½ oz) blueberries
icing (confectioners') sugar, to serve

Preheat the oven to 150°C (300°F/Gas 2). Line a baking tray with baking paper. Mark a 20 cm (8 inch) circle on the paper as a guide for the pavlova base.

Put the egg whites in a large, very clean, dry stainless steel or glass bowl—any hint of grease will prevent the egg whites foaming. Leave the whites for a few minutes to reach room temperature, then, using electric beaters, beat slowly until the whites start to become a frothy foam, then increase the speed until the bubbles in the foam have become small and even-sized. When the foam forms stiff peaks, add the sugar gradually, beating constantly after each addition, until the mixture is thick and glossy and all the sugar has dissolved. Don't overbeat or the mixture will become grainy.

Spread the mixture on the paper and shape it evenly into a circle, running a flat-bladed knife or spatula around the edge and over the top. Run the knife up the edge of the mixture, all the way around, to make furrows. This will strengthen the pavlova and give it a decorative finish.

Bake for 40 minutes, or until the pavlova is pale and crisp, then turn off the oven and cool in the oven with the door ajar. When cold, decorate with whipped cream, banana, raspberries and blueberries. Dust with sifted icing sugar before serving.

NOTE: The meringue can be cooked in advance and kept overnight in an airtight container. Serve the pavlova within 1 hour of decorating.

Summer pudding

SERVES 6   PREPARATION TIME 30 minutes plus overnight refrigeration   COOKING TIME 5 minutes

150 g (5½ oz) blackcurrants
150 g (5½ oz) redcurrants
150 g (5½ oz) raspberries
150 g (5½ oz) blackberries
200 g (7 oz) strawberries, hulled and quartered or halved
125 g (4½ oz/½ cup) caster (superfine) sugar, or to taste
6–8 slices good-quality sliced white bread, crusts removed

Put all of the berries, except the strawberries, in a large pan with 125 ml (4 fl oz/½ cup) water. Heat gently for 5 minutes, or until the berries begin to collapse. Add the strawberries and remove from the heat. Add the sugar, to taste (this will depend on how sweet the fruit is). Allow to cool.

Use the bread to line a 1 litre (35 fl oz/4 cup) pudding basin (steamed pudding mould) or six 170 ml (5½ fl oz/⅔ cup) moulds. For the large mould, cut a large circle out of one slice for the base. Cut the rest of the bread into wide fingers. For the small moulds, use one slice of bread for each, cutting a small circle to fit the base and strips to fit snugly around the sides. Drain a little of the juice off the fruit. Dip one side of each piece of bread into the juice before fitting it, juice side down, into the basin, leaving no gaps. Do not squeeze or flatten the bread or it will not absorb the juices.

Fill the centre of the basin with the fruit and add a little juice. Any fruit that doesn't fit in can be served with the pudding. Cover the top with the remaining dipped bread, juice side up, trimmed to fit. Cover with plastic wrap. Place a small plate which fits inside the dish onto the plastic wrap, then weigh it down with heavy cans. Place on a baking tray to catch any juices. For the small moulds, cover with plastic and sit a small can, or a similar weight, on top of each. Refrigerate overnight. Turn out the pudding/s and serve them with any leftover fruit mixture. This is delicious served with dollops of cream.

NOTE: If fresh berries aren't in season, use good-quality frozen berries. Thaw the berries on a tray in the refrigerator before using.

VINTAGE RIBBON
50 metres
house doctor
MERRY CHRISTMAS
MERRY CHRISTMAS
CHRISTMAS
LOL

Baking

Fruit cake

- MAKES 1
- PREPARATION TIME 20 minutes plus soaking
- COOKING TIME 3 hours 30 minutes

FRUIT MIXTURE

5 cups (800 g/1 lb 12 oz) sultanas (golden raisins)
2 cups (320 g/11¼ oz) raisins, chopped
1¼ cups (190 g/6¾ oz) currants
¾ cup (160 g/5½ oz) glacé (candied) cherries, quartered
250 g (9 oz) pitted prunes, quartered
125 g (4½ oz/⅔ cup) mixed peel (mixed candied citrus peel)
250 ml (9 fl oz/1 cup) brandy
3 tablespoons soft brown sugar
3 tablespoons sweet orange marmalade
1 tablespoon cocoa powder
2 teaspoons ground cinnamon
1 teaspoon ground ginger
1 teaspoon mixed (pumpkin pie) spice

250 g (9 oz) softened unsalted butter
230 g (8 oz/1 cup) soft brown sugar
2 teaspoons finely grated orange zest
2 teaspoons finely grated lemon zest
4 eggs
250 g (9 oz/2 cups) plain (all-purpose) flour, sifted
60 g (2¼ oz/½ cup) self-raising flour, sifted
whole blanched almonds, to decorate

To prepare the fruit mixture, mix the ingredients together in a large bowl, then store in a sterilised jar or airtight container in a cool, dark place for up to 1 month before using. Stir occasionally.

Lightly grease a 23 cm (9 inch) round or square cake tin. Cut a double layer of baking paper into a strip that is long enough to fit around the inside of the tin and tall enough to come 5 cm (2 inches) above the edge of the tin. Fold down a cuff about 2 cm (¾ inch) deep along the length of the strip, along the folded edges. Make diagonal cuts up to the fold line on each strip about 1 cm (½ inch) apart. Fit the strip around the inside of the tin, with the cuts on the base, pressing the cuts out at right angles so they sit flat around the base. Place the cake tin on a doubled piece of baking paper and draw around the edge. Cut it out and sit it on the base of the tin, over the cuts.

Preheat the oven to 150°C (300°F/Gas 2). Beat the butter, sugar and orange and lemon zests in a bowl with electric beaters until just combined. Add the eggs, one at a time, beating well after each addition. Transfer to a bowl and stir in half of the soaked fruit mixture alternately with the plain flour and the self-raising flour. Mix well, then spread evenly into the tin and tap the tin on the bench to remove any air bubbles. Dip your fingers in water and level the surface. Decorate the top of the cake with whole blanched almonds in a pattern.

Fold over several sheets of newspaper long enough to wrap around the side of the tin and to come a little higher than the baking paper. Tie around the tin securely with string and sit the tin on several layers of newspaper on the oven shelf. Bake for 3¼–3½ hours, or until a skewer comes out clean. Cover the top with baking paper, seal firmly with foil, then wrap the cake and tin in a clean tea towel (dish towel) and leave to cool.

Light fruit cake

MAKES 1 PREPARATION TIME 30 minutes
COOKING TIME 2 hours

- 185 g (6½ oz) unsalted butter, softened
- 115 g (4 oz/½ cup) caster (superfine) sugar
- 3 eggs
- 160 g (5½ oz/1 cup) sultanas (golden raisins)
- 100 g (3½ oz/⅔ cup) currants
- 3 tablespoons chopped glacé (candied) apricots
- 3 tablespoons chopped glacé (candied) figs
- 240 g (7½ oz/1 cup) chopped glacé (candied) cherries, plus extra, to decorate
- 80 g (2¾ oz/½ cup) macadamia nuts, coarsely chopped
- 185 g (6½ oz/1½ cups) plain (all-purpose) flour
- 60 g (2¼ oz/½ cup) self-raising flour
- 125 ml (4 fl oz/½ cup) milk
- 1 tablespoon sweet sherry

Preheat the oven to 160°C (315°F/Gas 2–3). Grease and line a deep 20 cm (8 inch) round or 18 cm (7 inch) square cake tin (see page 180).

Cream the butter and sugar in a bowl until just combined. Add the eggs, one at a time, beating well after each addition. Transfer the mixture to a bowl and stir in the fruit and nuts. Sift in half the flours and half the milk, stir to combine, then stir in the remaining flours and milk, and the sherry. Spoon into the prepared tin and tap the tin on the bench to remove any air bubbles. Smooth the surface with wet fingers and decorate the top with cherries. Wrap the outside of the tin in newspaper (see page 180). Sit the tin on several layers of newspaper in the oven and bake for 1¾–2 hours, until a skewer inserted into the centre comes out clean. The top may need to be covered with a sheet of baking paper if it colours too much.

Remove from the oven, remove the top baking paper and wrap the tin in a tea towel (dish towel) until cool. Remove the paper tin lining and store in an airtight container. Keeps for up to 2 weeks.

Boiled fruit cake

SERVES 8–10 PREPARATION TIME 30 minutes
COOKING TIME 1 hour 30 minutes

- 250 g (9 oz) unsalted butter
- 185 g (6½ oz/1 cup) soft brown sugar
- 1 kg (2 lb 4 oz) mixed dried fruit
- 125 ml (4 fl oz/½ cup) sweet sherry
- ½ teaspoon bicarbonate of soda (baking soda)
- 185 g (6½ oz/1½ cups) self-raising flour
- 125 g (4½ oz/1 cup) plain (all-purpose) flour
- 1 teaspoon ground mixed (pumpkin pie) spice
- 4 eggs, lightly beaten

Preheat the oven to 180°C (350°F/Gas 4). Lightly grease and line a 22 cm (8½ inch) round cake tin.

Put the butter, brown sugar, mixed fruit, sherry and 185 ml (6 fl oz/¾ cup) of water in a saucepan and stir over low heat until the butter has melted and the sugar has dissolved. Bring to the boil, then reduce the heat and simmer for 10 minutes. Remove from the heat, stir in the bicarbonate of soda and set aside to cool.

Sift the flours and spice into a large bowl and make a well in the centre. Add the egg to the fruit mixture, mix well, then pour into the well and mix thoroughly. Pour into the tin and smooth the surface. Wrap the outside of the tin in newspaper (see page 180). Sit the tin on several layers of newspaper in the oven.

Bake for 1–1¼ hours, until a skewer inserted into the centre of the cake comes out clean. Leave in the tin for at least an hour before turning out onto a wire rack to cool. The flavour improves after standing for 3 days.

NOTE: This cake can be kept for up to 2 months. The cake colour will depend on the fruit. For a dark cake, use raisins, currants and sultanas (golden raisins). For a lighter colour, mix in chopped glacé (candied) fruit.

Frosted fruit cake

MAKES 1
PREPARATION TIME 30 minutes plus overnight soaking
COOKING TIME 3 hours 30 minutes

640 g (1 lb 7 oz/4 cups) sultanas (golden raisins)
480 g (1 lb 1 oz/3 cups) raisins, chopped
300 g ($10\frac{1}{2}$ oz/2 cups) currants
265 g ($9\frac{1}{4}$ oz/$1\frac{1}{4}$ cups) glacé (candied) cherries, quartered
250 ml (9 fl oz/1 cup) brandy or rum
250 g (9 oz) unsalted butter, softened
230 g (8 oz/1 cup) dark brown sugar
2 tablespoons apricot jam (jelly)
2 tablespoons treacle or golden syrup
1 tablespoon grated lemon zest
4 eggs
340 g ($11\frac{3}{4}$ oz/$2\frac{3}{4}$ cups) plain (all-purpose) flour
1 teaspoon mixed (pumpkin pie) spice
1 teaspoon ground cinnamon
1 teaspoon ground ginger
1 tablespoon brandy or rum, extra

DECORATIONS
selection of seasonal fruits such as white and dark cherries, small bunches of red, white and black currants, apricots, tiny plums or pears
1 egg white
caster (superfine) sugar

ICING
1 egg white
1–3 teaspoons lemon juice
125 g ($4\frac{1}{2}$ oz/1 cup) pure icing (confectioners') sugar, sifted

Put the fruit in a large bowl with the brandy and leave to soak overnight.

Grease and line an oval cake tin 18 x 25 cm (7 x 10 inches), or a 23 cm (9 inch) round cake tin (see page 180). Preheat the oven to 150°C (300°F/Gas 2).

Beat the butter and brown sugar in a small bowl with electric beaters until just combined. Beat in the jam, treacle and zest. Add the eggs one at a time, beating well after each addition. Transfer to a large bowl.

Stir the fruit and the combined sifted flour and spices alternately into the mixture. Spoon the batter into the tin, tap the tin on the bench to remove any air bubbles and smooth the surface with wet fingers. Wrap the outside of the tin in newspaper (see page 180). Sit the tin on several layers of newspaper in the oven and bake for $3\frac{1}{4}$–$3\frac{1}{2}$ hours, or until a skewer inserted into the centre comes out clean. Drizzle with the extra brandy while hot. Cover the top with baking paper, cover tightly with foil and wrap the tin in a tea towel (dish towel) until the cake is completely cold.

Remove from the tin and store in an airtight container or wrapped in plastic wrap for up to 8 months.

Wash the fruit to be used for decorating several hours in advance so it is completely dry. Line a tray with paper towels.

Place the egg white in a shallow bowl and whisk until just foamy. Put some caster sugar on a large plate and, working with one portion of fruit at a time, brush the egg white lightly all over the fruit. Sprinkle the sugar over the fruit, shaking off any excess, and leave to dry on the paper-covered tray for about 1–2 hours, depending on the humidity. Frost more fruit than you think you will need so that you have a good selection.

To make the icing, whisk the egg white until just foamy, beat in 1 teaspoon of the lemon juice and then gradually beat in the icing (confectioners') sugar, beating well after each addition. The icing should be thick and white—add a little more lemon juice if necessary, but don't make it too runny. Place the fruit cake on a serving plate and, working quickly, pour the icing over the top. Using a palette knife, smooth the icing to the edge of the cake, allowing it to run slowly down the side of the cake. Leave for at least 10 minutes to let the icing set a little before arranging the frosted fruits on the top. The iced cake will keep for up to a month.

Glacé fruit and nut loaf

SERVES 12 PREPARATION TIME 30 minutes
COOKING TIME 1 hour 45 minutes

50 g (1¾ oz) butter, softened
3 tablespoons soft brown sugar
2 tablespoons breakfast marmalade
2 eggs
125 g (4½ oz/1 cup) plain (all-purpose) flour
1 teaspoon baking powder
1 teaspoon ground nutmeg
200 g (7 oz/1¼ cups) pitted dried dates
240 g (8½ oz/1½ cups) raisins, chopped
140 g (5 oz/⅔ cup) red, yellow and green glacé (candied) cherries, quartered
110 g (3¾ oz/½ cup) chopped glacé (candied) pear or pineapple
120 g (4¼ oz/½ cup) chopped glacé (candied) apricots
120 g (4¼ oz/½ cup) chopped glacé (candied) peaches
120 g (4¼ oz/⅓ cup) chopped glacé (candied) figs
155 g (5½ oz/1 cup) brazil nuts
100 g (3½ oz/1 cup) walnut halves
100 g (3½ oz/⅔ cup) blanched almonds

TOPPING
2 teaspoons gelatine
2 tablespoons breakfast marmalade
150 g (5½ oz) glacé (candied) pineapple or pear rings
100 g (3½ oz) red, yellow and green glacé (candied) cherries
3 tablespoons blanched almonds, toasted

Grease a deep 20.5 x 8 cm (8 x 3 inch) bar tin and line the base and sides with baking paper. Preheat the oven to 150°C (300°F/Gas 2).

Beat the butter, sugar and marmalade together until pale and creamy. Add the eggs and beat until combined.

Sift the flour, baking powder and nutmeg into a large bowl. Add the fruit and nuts and mix until each piece is coated in the flour. Add to the egg mixture and mix until combined.

Put the mixture in the bar tin, pushing well into each corner. Bake for 1½–1¾ hours, or until a skewer inserted into the centre comes out clean. Cool in the tin for 10 minutes before turning out. Remove the baking paper and transfer to a wire rack to cool.

For the topping, sprinkle the gelatine over 2 tablespoons water and the marmalade in a small heatproof bowl. Bring a pan of water to the boil, then remove from the heat. Stand the bowl in the pan and stir until the gelatine has dissolved. Brush the top of the cake with some of the gelatine mixture and top with the pineapple, cherries and almonds. Brush or drizzle with more gelatine mixture and allow to set.

NOTE: This type of cake is known in some places as an American-style fruit cake, or a stained-glass fruit cake.

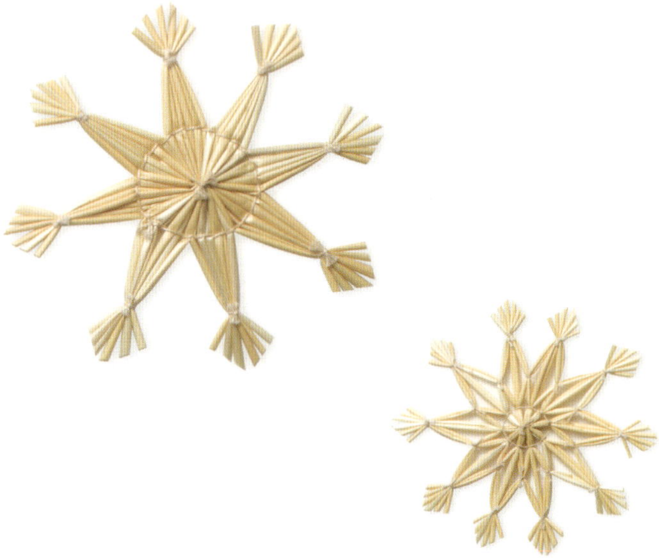

Black bun

MAKES 1 PREPARATION TIME 45 minutes plus chilling
COOKING TIME 2 hours 30 minutes

310 g (11 oz/2½ cups) plain (all-purpose) flour
½ teaspoon baking powder
150 g (5½ oz) butter, chilled and grated
1 egg, beaten

FILLING
90 g (3¼ oz/¾ cup) plain (all-purpose) flour
½ teaspoon freshly grated nutmeg
½ teaspoon ground coriander
½ teaspoon mixed (pumpkin pie) spice
1 teaspoon ground cinnamon
1 teaspoon ground ginger
115 g (4 oz/½ cup) soft brown sugar
590 g (1 lb 5 oz/3⅔ cups) raisins, chopped
240 g (8½ oz/1½ cups) sultanas (golden raisins)
350 g (12 oz/2⅓ cups) currants
95 g (3¼ oz/½ cup) mixed peel (mixed candied citrus peel)
100 g (3½ oz/⅔ cup) blanched almonds, chopped
2 teaspoons finely grated lemon zest
2 eggs
2 tablespoons brandy
3 tablespoons treacle
2 tablespoons milk

Grease a 24 cm (9 inch) springform cake tin. Sift the flour, baking powder and ¼ teaspoon salt into a bowl. Mix the butter into the flour with your fingertips. Make a well, add up to 80 ml (2½ fl oz/⅓ cup) water and mix with a flat-bladed knife, using a cutting action, until the mixture comes together in clumps (you may need extra water). Gather together and lift onto a lightly floured surface. Press into a ball, cover with plastic wrap and refrigerate for 30 minutes.

Divide the dough into three portions. Roll out one portion, on a lightly floured surface, to fit the base of the tin. Divide another portion into thirds and roll each piece to line the side of the tin. Refrigerate the tin and the remaining portion of dough while preparing the filling.

Preheat the oven to 150°C (300°F/Gas 2). To make the filling, sift the flour, spices and ¼ teaspoon salt into a large bowl, then stir in the sugar, fruit, peel, almonds and zest. Mix well.

Lightly beat the eggs with the brandy, treacle and milk in a bowl, then mix into the fruit. The mixture should come together, but not be too wet.

Spoon the filling into the pastry-lined tin and press into the base. The mixture will only come about three-quarters up the sides. Fold the pastry edges over the filling and brush the pastry with beaten egg. Roll out the remaining pastry, on a lightly floured surface, until large enough to cover the top. Trim to fit and press down firmly to seal. Prick the pastry top a few times with a fork. Brush with the beaten egg and bake for 2–2½ hours. The top should be golden brown. If the pastry is over-browning, cover loosely with foil. Place the tin on a wire rack for 20 minutes to cool, then remove the side of the springform tin, and cool completely. When cold, store in an airtight container. Serve cut into wedges.

Fruit mince pies

MAKES 24 PREPARATION TIME 30 minutes
COOKING TIME 25 minutes

FRUIT MINCE
40 g (1½ oz/⅓ cup) raisins, chopped
60 g (2¼ oz/⅓ cup) soft brown sugar
3 tablespoons sultanas (golden raisins)
3 tablespoons mixed peel (mixed candied citrus peel)
1 tablespoon currants
1 tablespoon chopped almonds
1 small apple, grated
1 teaspoon lemon juice
½ teaspoon finely grated orange zest
½ teaspoon finely grated lemon zest
½ teaspoon mixed (pumpkin pie) spice
pinch freshly grated nutmeg
25 g (1 oz) unsalted butter, melted
1 tablespoon brandy

PASTRY
250 g (9 oz/2 cups) plain (all-purpose) flour
150 g (5½ oz) chilled unsalted butter, cubed
85 g (3 oz/⅔ cup) icing (confectioners') sugar
2–3 tablespoons iced water

icing (confectioners') sugar, to dust

To make the fruit mince, combine all the ingredients in a bowl, spoon into a sterilised jar and seal. You can use the fruit mince straight away but the flavours develop if kept for a while. Keep it in a cool dark place for up to 3 months. (Use ready-made fruit mince if you are short of time.)

Preheat the oven to 180°C (350°F/Gas 4). Lightly grease two 12-hole shallow patty pans or mini muffin tins.

To make the pastry, sift the flour into a bowl. Using your fingertips, rub in the butter until the mixture resembles fine breadcrumbs. Stir in the icing sugar and make a well in the centre. Add almost all the water and mix with a flat-bladed knife, using a cutting action, until the mixture just comes together in beads. Add the remaining water if the dough is too dry. Turn out onto a lightly floured work surface and gather into a ball. Roll out two-thirds of the pastry and cut out 24 rounds, slightly larger than the holes in the tins, with a round fluted cutter. Fit the rounds into the tins.

Divide the fruit mince evenly among the pastry cases. Roll out the remaining pastry, a little thinner than before, and cut 12 rounds with the same cutter. Using a smaller fluted cutter, cut 12 more rounds. Place the large circles on top of half the pies and press the edges to seal. Place the smaller circles on the remainder. Bake for 25 minutes, or until golden. Leave in the tins for 5 minutes, then lift out with a knife and cool on wire racks. Dust lightly with icing sugar.

Spicy fruit biscuits

MAKES about 60 PREPARATION TIME 30 minutes plus chilling
COOKING TIME 15 minutes

180 g (6½ oz) unsalted butter, softened
185 g (6½ oz/1 cup) soft brown sugar
1 teaspoon natural vanilla extract
1 egg
280 g (10 oz/2¼ cups) plain (all-purpose) flour
1 teaspoon baking powder
1 teaspoon ground mixed (pumpkin pie) spice
½ teaspoon ground ginger
95 g (3¼ oz/½ cup) fruit mince (mincemeat)

Cream the butter and sugar in a small bowl using electric beaters until light and fluffy. Add the vanilla extract and egg and beat until well combined. Transfer to a large bowl and add the sifted flour, baking powder, mixed spice and ground ginger. Using a flat-bladed knife, mix to a soft dough. Gather together, then divide the mixture into two portions. Roll one portion out on a sheet of baking paper to a rectangle about 2 mm (1/16 inch) thick and trim the edges. Repeat with the other portion of dough. Refrigerate until just firm.

Spread both portions of dough with the fruit mince and then carefully roll up Swiss-roll-style (jelly-roll-style). Refrigerate for 30 minutes, or until firm.

Preheat the oven to 180°C (350°F/Gas 4). Line two baking trays with baking paper. Cut the logs into slices 1 cm (½ inch) thick. Place on the prepared trays, leaving 3 cm (1¼ inches) between each slice. Bake for 10–15 minutes, or until golden. Cool on the trays for 3 minutes before transferring to a wire rack to cool completely. Store in an airtight container.

Fruit mince slice

MAKES 15 PREPARATION TIME 20 minutes plus chilling
COOKING TIME 40 minutes

250 g (9 oz/2 cups) plain (all-purpose) flour
60 g (2¼ oz/½ cup) icing (confectioners') sugar
185 g (6½ oz) unsalted butter, cubed
1 egg
410 g (14½ oz) fruit mince (mincemeat)
150 g (5½ oz) pitted prunes, chopped
100 g (3½ oz) glacé (candied) ginger, chopped
1 egg, lightly beaten
icing (confectioners') sugar, extra, to dust

Preheat the oven to 190°C (375°F/Gas 5). Lightly grease a shallow 18 x 28 cm (7 x 11¼ inch) tin and line the base with baking paper, leaving the paper hanging over the two long sides. Sift the flour and icing sugar into a large bowl. Rub in the butter with your fingertips until the mixture resembles fine breadcrumbs. Make a well in the centre and add the egg. Mix with a flat-bladed knife, using a cutting action, until the mixture comes together. Turn onto a lightly floured surface and press together until smooth.

Divide the dough in half and press one portion into the tin. Bake for 10 minutes, then leave to cool. Roll the remaining pastry out on a piece of baking paper and refrigerate for 15 minutes. Spread the fruit mince evenly over the baked pastry, topping with the prunes and ginger.

Cut the rolled pastry into thin strips with a sharp knife or fluted pastry wheel. Arrange the strips on top of the fruit in a diagonal lattice pattern. Brush with the beaten egg. Bake for 30 minutes, or until golden. Cool in the tin, then lift out, using the paper as handles, and cut into squares or fingers. Serve dusted with icing sugar. The slice can be kept for up to 4 days if stored in an airtight container in a cool place, or in the refrigerator.

Stollen

SERVES 10–12 PREPARATION TIME 40 minutes plus soaking and rising COOKING TIME 40 minutes

180 g (6¼ oz) raisins
2½ tablespoons dark rum
160 ml (5¼ fl oz) milk, warmed
2 teaspoons dried yeast
3 tablespoons caster (superfine) sugar
50 g (1¾ oz/⅓ cup) chopped blanched almonds
625 g (1 lb 6 oz/5 cups) plain (all-purpose) flour
¼ teaspoon ground cardamom
¼ teaspoon freshly grated nutmeg
¼ teaspoon ground cinnamon
250 g (9 oz/1 cup) unsalted butter, cut into cubes and softened
1 egg
50 g (1¾ oz) finely chopped glacé (candied) orange
1 teaspoon finely grated lemon zest
50 g (1¾ oz) unsalted butter, extra, melted
60 g (2¼ oz/½ cup) icing (confectioners') sugar, sifted

Place the raisins in a bowl, add the rum and mix well. Cover and set aside to soak overnight, then drain.

The next day, combine the milk, yeast and 1 tablespoon of the caster sugar in a small bowl. Set aside in a warm place for 10 minutes, or until frothy. Soak the almonds in boiling water for 10 minutes, then drain.

Sift the flour, spices and the remaining caster sugar into a large bowl and make a well in the centre. Pour in the yeast mixture, add the butter and egg and mix with your hands until the dough just comes together. Turn out onto a lightly floured work surface and knead for 10–12 minutes, or until the dough is spongy and elastic. Sprinkle the dough with the raisins, glacé orange, lemon zest and almonds and knead until soft and smooth. Transfer the dough to a large greased bowl and cover with plastic wrap. Place the bowl in a warm spot for 1½–2 hours, or until doubled in size.

Turn the dough out onto a lightly floured work surface, and knead and punch the dough, knocking all the air out of it. Shape into a 15 x 30 cm (6 x 12 inch) log, then wrap in foil (this helps the stollen keep its shape and prevents it from becoming flattened). Transfer the log to a baking tray, cover with a clean tea towel (dish towel) and set aside in a warm place for 30 minutes, or until light and puffy once more.

Preheat the oven to 180°C (350°F/Gas 4). Remove the foil and bake the stollen for 35–40 minutes, or until golden and well risen. Brush the top with the melted butter and dust with icing sugar. Transfer to a wire rack to cool completely. Cut into 1 cm (½ inch) thick slices to serve.

NOTES: Stollen is a rich fruit bread from Germany. The oval shape represents the Christ Child in swaddling clothes. It will keep, covered in foil and plastic wrap, in the refrigerator for up to 2 weeks.

Yule log

SERVES 8 PREPARATION TIME 40 minutes
COOKING TIME 15 minutes

60 g (2¼ oz/½ cup) plain (all-purpose) flour
2 tablespoons cocoa powder
3 eggs
90 g (3¼ oz/⅓ cup) caster (superfine) sugar
50 g (1¾ oz) butter, melted and cooled
1 tablespoon caster (superfine) sugar, extra

FILLING
125 g (4½ oz) white chocolate, chopped
125 ml (4 fl oz/½ cup) cream
50 g (1¾ oz) hazelnuts, toasted and finely chopped

TOPPING
125 g (4½ oz) dark chocolate, chopped
125 ml (4 fl oz/½ cup) cream, extra, for topping
icing (confectioners') sugar, to dust

Grease a 30 x 35 cm (12 x 14 inch) Swiss roll tin and line the base and sides with baking paper. Preheat the oven to 180°C (350°F/Gas 4).

Sift the flour and cocoa powder together twice. Using electric beaters, beat the eggs and sugar for 5 minutes, or until light and fluffy and increased in volume. Sift the flour over the egg mixture and pour the butter around the edge of the bowl. Use a large metal spoon to gently fold the mixture together to incorporate the flour and butter. Take care not to overmix and lose too much volume.

Spread the mixture into the tin and bake for 12 minutes, or until the sponge springs back when lightly touched with your fingertips. Sprinkle the extra caster sugar over a clean tea towel (dish towel). Turn the sponge out onto the towel close to one end. Roll the sponge and towel together lengthways and leave to cool.

For the filling, put the white chocolate in a small heatproof bowl. Bring a small pan of water to the boil, then remove from the heat. Add the cream to the chocolate and stand the bowl over the pan of water, making sure the base of the bowl does not touch the water, until the chocolate is soft. Stir until smooth. Leave the mixture until it has cooled to room temperature and is the consistency of cream.

Repeat with the dark chocolate and cream for the topping. Leave the mixture until it cools to a spreadable consistency.

Beat the white chocolate mixture with electric beaters until soft peaks form—do not overbeat or the mixture will curdle. Unroll the sponge and remove the towel. Spread the filling over the sponge, finishing about 2 cm (¾ inch) from the end. Sprinkle with the hazelnuts. Re-roll the sponge and trim the ends. Cut off one end on the diagonal and place it alongside the log to create a branch.

Place the yule log on a serving plate and spread the topping all over it. Run the tines of a fork along the roll to give a 'bark' effect. Just before serving, dust with icing sugar. Decorate with some fresh green leaves and red berries.

Gingerbread house

If you are feeling creative and like a challenge, delight your family with an attractive gingerbread house that can be decorated as simply or intricately as you wish.

MAKING THE MIXTURE

Using electric beaters, beat 250 g (9 oz) softened unsalted butter, 155 g (5½ oz/⅔ cup) soft brown sugar and 175 ml (5½ fl oz/⅔ cup) of golden syrup until light and creamy. Gradually add 2 lightly beaten eggs and beat thoroughly after each addition. Sift 625 g (1 lb 6 oz/5 cups) of plain (all-purpose) flour, 2 tablespoons of ground ginger and 2 teaspoons of bicarbonate of soda into the bowl and stir until combined. Bring the dough together with your hands, turn it out onto a well-floured surface, then knead until smooth. Cover and refrigerate for 30 minutes.

CUTTING THE SHAPES

Meanwhile, cut a paper pattern for each part of the house (when cutting the gingerbread you will need to cut out two pieces from each paper pattern). The pattern for the sides should measure 10 x 20 cm (4 x 8 inches), the roof 15 x 20 cm (6 x 8 inches) and the front/back 16 x 20 cm (6½ x 8 inches). Measure 10 cm (4 inches) down from the centre of the front/back piece and then draw a line across the rectangle. Turn the paper so that the smaller rectangle is at the top, then draw a diagonal line from the centre of the top of the rectangle across to each side, joining with the line already drawn across (this will give you a triangular end to the rectangle), then cut off the corners. Preheat the oven to 180°C (350°F/Gas 4). Roll out the dough between two sheets of baking paper, in two batches if necessary, to 5 mm (¼ inch) thick. Using the templates as a

guide, cut out two roof pieces, a front and back piece and two sides of the house. Cut 4 rectangular pieces for the chimney 5 x 4 cm (2 x 1½ inches), then cut a wedge out of two of them so they will sit on the roof when joined together. If you would like windows or a door, cut these from the gingerbread. Line four baking trays with baking paper. Lift the pieces onto the trays and refrigerate for 20 minutes, then bake each tray for 12 minutes. Set aside to cool. For the stained-glass windows, crush assorted coloured boiled sweets and use them to fill the cut-out windows about 5 minutes before the gingerbread is cooked. They will melt together.

ICING AND ASSEMBLY

Place 1 egg white in a bowl and gradually add about 280 g (10 oz/2¼ cups) of sifted pure icing (confectioners') sugar until you have a smooth mixture that will stay in place when piped—if it is too runny, add more icing sugar. To assemble the house, join the front and sides of the house together with a piped line of icing and leave them to dry. Add the back to the house in the same way, hold for a few minutes, then stand up to dry. Decorate the outside seam with more piped icing to strengthen it. Join the chimney pieces together with a little icing. Attach the roof pieces and chimney using more piped icing. Leave everything to dry before decorating. Decorate the roof by attaching sweets with icing or piping decorations such as roof tiles or ivy onto the house.

NOTE: Extra mixture can be made and cut into tree shapes to decorate the scene. This quantity of mixture is also enough to make about 30 gingerbread people.

Panforte

SERVES 10–12 PREPARATION TIME 20 minutes
COOKING TIME 40 minutes

- 100 g (3½ oz/⅔ cup) blanched almonds
- 105 g (3½ oz/¾ cup) hazelnuts, toasted and skinned
- 95 g (3¼ oz/½ cup) mixed peel (mixed candied citrus peel), chopped
- 110 g (3¾ oz/½ cup) chopped glacé (candied) pineapple
- 3 tablespoons unsweetened cocoa powder
- 60 g (2¼ oz/½ cup) plain (all-purpose) flour
- ½ teaspoon ground cinnamon
- ¼ teaspoon mixed (pumpkin pie) spice
- 75 g (2¾ oz/⅓ cup) sugar
- 115 g (4 oz/⅓ cup) honey
- icing (confectioners') sugar, sifted, for dusting

Grease and line a 20 cm (8 inch) springform cake tin with baking paper.

Toast the almonds under a hot grill (broiler) until golden, then set aside to cool. Place the toasted almonds and hazelnuts in a heatproof bowl, add the mixed peel, pineapple, cocoa, flour and spices and toss well.

Preheat the oven to 150°C (300°F/Gas 2).

Combine the sugar and the honey in a small heavy-based saucepan and cook over low heat until the sugar dissolves. Continue to cook until the syrup reaches the soft ball stage (the mixture should be soft and pliable when dropped into cold water and pressed between your finger and thumb) and turns from golden to brown in colour.

Pour the syrup onto the nut mixture and, working quickly, mix well before it hardens. Spoon into the tin, pressing down firmly, and smooth the surface. Bake for 35 minutes. Unlike other cakes this will neither firm up nor colour as it cooks, so you need to time it carefully.

Cool in the tin until the cake is firm enough to allow you to remove the side of the tin. Peel off the lining paper, and set aside to cool completely. Dust the top heavily with the icing sugar before serving.

NOTE: This fruity, spicy, dense-textured flat cake originated in Siena, Tuscany. It can be stored, wrapped in baking paper and foil and refrigerated, for up to 6 weeks.

Panettone

MAKES 1 PREPARATION TIME 30 minutes plus rising
COOKING TIME 50 minutes

90 g (3¼ oz/½ cup) mixed peel (mixed candied citrus peel)
80 g (2¾ oz/½ cup) sultanas (golden raisins)
1 teaspoon grated lemon zest
1 teaspoon grated orange zest
1 tablespoon brandy or rum
7 g (¼ oz) sachet dried yeast
220 ml (7½ fl oz) warm milk
3 tablespoons caster (superfine) sugar
400 g (14 oz/3¼ cups) white strong flour
2 eggs
1 teaspoon natural vanilla extract
150 g (5½ oz) unsalted butter, softened
20 g (½ oz) unsalted butter, melted, to glaze

Put the mixed peel, sultanas and grated zest in a small bowl. Add the alcohol, mix well and set aside.

Put the yeast, warm milk and 1 teaspoon sugar in a small bowl and leave in a warm place for 10–15 minutes, or until foamy. Sift 200 g (7 oz) flour and ½ teaspoon salt into a large bowl, make a well in the centre and add the yeast mixture. Mix with a large metal spoon to form a soft dough. Cover the bowl and leave to 'sponge' and rise in a warm place for 45 minutes, or until frothy and risen.

Add the eggs, the remaining sugar and vanilla and mix. Add the butter and stir until well combined. Stir in the remaining flour and mix well. Knead well on a floured surface until the dough is smooth and elastic. You may need to add up to 60 g (2¼ oz/½ cup) flour to the dough as you knead. Place the dough in a lightly greased bowl, cover with plastic wrap and leave in a warm place for 1½–2 hours, or until doubled.

Lightly grease a 15 cm (6 inch) round cake tin and line the base and side with a double thickness of baking paper. Ensure the collar extends above the rim of the tin by 10 cm (4 inches).

Knock back the dough and turn out onto a floured surface. Roll into a 30 x 20 cm (12 x 8 inch) rectangle. Drain the fruit mixture and spread half the fruit over the dough. Fold over the short edges like an envelope to cover the fruit. Roll again and repeat the process to incorporate all the fruit. Gently knead the dough for 2–3 minutes and shape into a neat ball. Place in the tin, brush with the melted butter, then slash a cross on the top with a sharp knife and leave to rise again in a warm place for 45 minutes, or until doubled in size.

Preheat the oven to 190°C (375°F/Gas 5) and bake for 50 minutes, or until the panettone is golden brown and a skewer inserted into the centre comes out clean. Leave in the tin for 5 minutes, then transfer to a wire rack to cool.

NOTE: This yeast cake is a speciality of Milan but it is enjoyed throughout Italy at festive times such as Christmas and Easter.

Gingerbread stars

MAKES 48
PREPARATION TIME 40 minutes, plus 30 minutes chilling
COOKING TIME 10 minutes per tray

150 g (5½ oz) butter, softened
115 g (4 oz/½ cup) caster (superfine) sugar
3 tablespoons honey
1 egg
340 g (11¾ oz/2¾ cups) plain (all-purpose) flour
½ teaspoon baking powder
1 teaspoon bicarbonate of soda (baking soda)
1 teaspoon ground cinnamon
1 tablespoon ground ginger
silver cachous, to decorate

GLACE ICING
185 g (6½ oz/1½ cups) icing (confectioners') sugar
½ teaspoon softened butter
2–2½ tablespoons boiling water

ROYAL ICING
1 egg white
185 g (6½ oz/1½ cups) icing (confectioners') sugar
½–1 teaspoon lemon juice

Cream the butter, sugar and honey in a large bowl using electric beaters until pale and fluffy. Add the egg and beat well. Sift in the flour, baking powder, bicarbonate of soda, cinnamon and ginger. Stir until the mixture comes together to form a ball. Turn out onto a lightly floured work surface and gently knead until smooth. Cover with plastic wrap and refrigerate for 30 minutes.

Preheat the oven to 180°C (350°F/Gas 4). Line two baking trays with baking paper.

Roll out the dough on a lightly floured surface to 2 mm (1/16 inch) thick. Cut the dough into star shapes with a 7 cm (2¾ inch) star-shaped cookie cutter, re-rolling any dough scraps and cutting out more stars. Place on the prepared trays, leaving room for a little spreading, and bake for 6 minutes, or until lightly browned. Allow to cool on the trays for 2 minutes, then transfer to a wire rack to cool completely.

To make the glacé icing, combine the icing sugar, butter and boiling water in a small heatproof bowl and mix to a smooth paste. Place the bowl over a small saucepan of simmering water and stir until warm and the consistency of whipping cream. Do not overheat. Dip the top of each star into the icing and allow the excess to drip off. Leave on a wire rack to set.

To make the royal icing, lightly whisk the egg white in a small bowl until just foamy. Gradually whisk in enough icing sugar and lemon juice to form a smooth icing that holds its shape. Spoon the icing into a piping (icing) bag fitted with a small 2 mm (1/16 inch) plain nozzle (or use a small plastic bag and snip off a small corner) and pipe decorations onto the gingerbread stars. Decorate with silver cachous if desired. Allow to set.

Speculaas

MAKES about 48 PREPARATION TIME 20 minutes plus 45 minutes refrigeration COOKING TIME 12 minutes per tray

- 405 g ($14\frac{1}{4}$ oz/$3\frac{1}{4}$ cups) plain (all-purpose) flour
- 1 teaspoon ground cinnamon
- $\frac{1}{4}$ teaspoon ground nutmeg
- $\frac{1}{4}$ teaspoon ground cloves
- $\frac{1}{4}$ teaspoon ground cardamom
- 160 g ($5\frac{3}{4}$ oz) unsalted butter, softened
- 310 g (11 oz/$1\frac{1}{3}$ cups) soft brown sugar
- 1 egg
- 80 ml ($2\frac{1}{2}$ fl oz/$\frac{1}{3}$ cup) milk
- 3 tablespoons ground almonds
- milk, extra, for glazing

Preheat the oven to 200°C (400°F/Gas 6). Cover baking trays with baking paper. Sift the flour, spices and $\frac{1}{4}$ teaspoon salt together into a large bowl.

Beat the butter and sugar together in a bowl until pale and creamy. Beat in the egg, mixing well, and then the milk. Fold in the almonds, then the sifted flour and spices and mix well. Wrap in plastic and refrigerate for 45 minutes.

Divide the mixture into four portions and roll each portion out on a lightly floured surface to 4 mm ($\frac{1}{8}$ inch) thick. Cut into shapes using Christmas-theme cutters (stars, trees or bells). Place on the baking trays, leaving room for spreading. Brush with milk and bake for 12 minutes, or until light brown. Repeat with the remaining dough, chilling any scraps before re-rolling. Cool the biscuits on wire racks. When cold, store in airtight containers.

NOTE: This Christmas biscuit is from the Rhine area in Germany and neighbouring Holland.

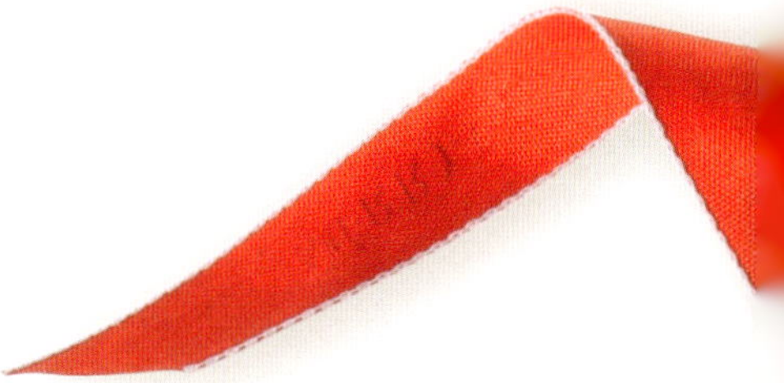

Cinnamon stars

MAKES about 30 PREPARATION TIME 15 minutes plus chilling
COOKING TIME 10 minutes per tray

- 2 egg whites
- 280 g (10 oz/2¼ cups) icing (confectioners') sugar
- 145 g (5 oz/1½ cups) ground almonds
- 1½ tablespoons ground cinnamon

Beat the egg whites lightly with a wooden spoon in a large bowl. Gradually stir in the sifted icing sugar to form a smooth paste. Remove 100 g (3½ oz/⅓ cup) of the mixture, cover and set aside. Add the ground almonds and cinnamon to the remaining icing and gently press together with your hands. Add 1 teaspoon water if the mixture is too dry. Press together well before adding any water as the warmth of your hands will soften the mixture.

Lightly dust a work surface with icing sugar and roll out the mixture to about 3 mm (⅛ inch) thick. Spread with a thin layer of the reserved icing. Leave, uncovered, at room temperature for 30–35 minutes, or until the icing has set.

Preheat the oven to 150°C (300°F/Gas 2). Line two baking trays with baking paper. Cut out shapes using a star cutter (about 5 cm/2 inches across from point to point). Dip the cutter in icing sugar to help prevent sticking. Place the stars on the trays and cook for 10 minutes, or until just firm. Turn the tray around after 5 minutes. Cool on the tray. Store in an airtight container for up to 2 weeks.

STAR DECORATION

This simple star shape, propped up on a mantelpiece, window ledge or shelf, makes a lovely Christmas decoration.

The project uses white willow tied with white willow rods, though it would also be effective made in other colours, or perhaps with contrasting ties. You could also spray paint the finished form in silver, bronze, copper or gold.

YOU WILL NEED

To make a decoration with a diameter of 26 cm (10½ inches):

- 30 lengths of white willow, each measuring 92 cm (36½ inches)
- Damp tea towel
- Pair of sharp secateurs
- Bradawl, bodkin or knitting needle

Soak 12 or 13 willow rods in a bath of cold water for 1 hour, then wrap them in a damp tea towel (dish towel) and set aside. With the secateurs, cut the dry willow into 35 lengths, each 26 cm (10½ inches) long. Divide these into five bundles, with seven sticks in each.

Take the first and second bundles, place the end of the first bundle on top of the end of the second bundle and hold at a 45-degree angle. Bind the bundles together by sliding the thin end (tip) of one of the wet willow rods through both bundles about 2 cm (¾ inch) from the top.

Wrap the wet rod three times around the two bundles and slide the thick end (butt) through the bind. It may help to use a bradawl to ease it through. Pull tightly to make it secure.

Trim the ends of the willow neatly with the secateurs, so that the points of the star are even. Make sure you do not trim too close to the binding or you could weaken the joints. Take a third bundle and place over the other end of the second bundle. Hold at a 45-degree angle. Bind the ends together as before and trim them.

Take a fourth bundle and place over the other end of the third bundle—it should be placed across, over the first bundle and under the second bundle. Bind and trim as before. Bind the fifth bundle to the ends of bundles one and four, running over two and under three.

Arrange the star so it looks even. Then bind each of the cross sections—take a wet willow rod and slide the tip through the cross section so that it holds. Bring the butt up through the hole in the middle of the star and continue to wrap three times. Slide the butt through the bind and pull tight. Trim off all ends neatly.

Chocolate pfeffernusse

MAKES 65 PREPARATION TIME 50 minutes plus 2 hours refrigeration COOKING TIME 15 minutes per tray

- 200 ml (7 fl oz) honey
- 100 ml (3½ fl oz) treacle
- 155 g (5½ oz/⅔ cup) soft brown sugar
- 150 g (5½ oz) unsalted butter
- 500 g (1 lb 2 oz/4 cups) plain (all-purpose) flour
- 60 g (2¼ oz/½ cup) cocoa powder
- 1 teaspoon baking powder
- ½ teaspoon bicarbonate of soda (baking soda)
- 1 teaspoon ground white pepper
- 1 teaspoon ground cinnamon
- ½ teaspoon freshly grated nutmeg
- 100 g (3½ oz/⅔ cup) almonds, chopped
- 1 teaspoon finely grated lemon zest
- 3 tablespoons mixed peel (mixed candied citrus peel)
- 2 eggs, lightly beaten
- 300 g (10½ oz) dark chocolate, chopped

Put the honey, treacle, brown sugar and butter in a saucepan over medium heat and bring to the boil. Remove the pan from the heat and set aside until cool. Sift the flour, cocoa, baking powder, bicarbonate of soda, spices and ¼ teaspoon salt into a large bowl. Stir in the almonds, lemon zest and mixed peel. Make a well in the centre. Pour in the honey mixture and the eggs and mix. Cover and refrigerate for 2 hours.

Preheat the oven to 180°C (350°F/Gas 4). Cover two baking trays with baking paper.

Roll level tablespoons of the dough into balls. Place on the trays. Bake for 12–15 minutes, until firm to the touch. Allow to cool.

To decorate, put the chocolate in a heatproof bowl. Bring a saucepan of water to the boil, then remove from the heat. Sit the bowl over the pan, making sure the base of the bowl doesn't sit in the water. Stir occasionally until the chocolate melts. Dip the tops of the biscuits in the chocolate, allow the excess to drain off, then place on baking paper to set.

NOTE: Pfeffernusse are a German Christmas treat.

Stained-glass window biscuits

MAKES about 20 PREPARATION TIME 1 hour plus 15 minutes refrigeration COOKING TIME 10 minutes

150 g (5½ oz) unsalted butter, cubed, softened
60 g (2¼ oz/½ cup) icing (confectioners') sugar
1 egg
1 teaspoon natural vanilla extrac
40 g (1⅓ oz/⅓ cup) custard powder
250 g (9 oz/2 cups) plain (all-purpose) flour
3 tablespoons self-raising flour
200 g (7 oz) assorted boiled sweets
beaten egg, to glaze

Line two baking trays with baking paper. Beat the butter and icing sugar until light and creamy. Add the egg and the vanilla and beat until fluffy, then beat in the custard powder. Fold in the combined sifted flours.

Turn the dough onto a lightly floured surface and knead until smooth. Roll between 2 sheets of baking paper to a thickness of 3 mm (⅛ inch). Refrigerate for 15 minutes, or until firm.

Preheat the oven to 200°C (400°F/Gas 6). Separate the boiled sweets into their different colours and crush using a rolling pin. Cut the biscuit dough into rounds using a 9.5 cm (3½ inch) fluted cutter. Lay on the trays. Use small cutters to cut shapes from inside the circles.

Glaze the biscuits with beaten egg and bake for 5 minutes. Don't let the glaze drip into the cutout sections of the biscuits or the stained glass will be cloudy. Fill each cut-out section with a different-coloured sweet. Bake for 5–6 minutes, or until the sweets melt. Leave for 10 minutes, then cool on a wire rack.

Passionfruit curd

MAKES 750 ml (26 fl oz/3 cups) PREPARATION TIME 15 minutes COOKING TIME 20 minutes

4 eggs
185 g (6½ oz/¾ cup) caster (superfine) sugar
80 ml (2½ fl oz/⅓ cup) lemon juice
3 teaspoons finely grated lemon zest
125 g (4½ oz/½ cup) passionfruit pulp
200 g (7 oz) unsalted butter, chopped

Beat the eggs well, then strain into a heatproof bowl. Stir in the sugar, lemon juice, lemon zest, passionfruit pulp and butter. Place the bowl over a saucepan of simmering water and stir constantly with a wooden spoon over low heat for about 15–20 minutes, or until the butter has melted and the mixture thickly coats the back of the wooden spoon.

Pour the passionfruit curd into clean, warm jars and seal while hot. Turn upside down for 2 minutes, then invert and cool. Refrigerate for up to 1 month.

Shortbread bells

MAKES about 40 PREPARATION TIME 30 minutes plus 15 minutes refrigeration COOKING TIME 25 minutes

250 g (9 oz) butter, softened
125 g (4½ oz/½ cup) caster (superfine) sugar
250 g (9 oz/2 cups) plain (all-purpose) flour
90 g (3¼ oz/½ cup) rice flour
1 egg white, lightly beaten
edible gold leaf (see Note)

Line two baking trays with baking paper. Beat the butter and sugar with electric beaters until light and creamy.

Sift the flours into the butter mixture, and mix together with a flat-bladed knife to make a crumbly dough. Gather together and turn the dough out onto a sheet of baking paper. Press together gently. Cover with another sheet of baking paper and roll out to 7 mm (¼ inch) thick.

Peel off the top sheet of baking paper and cut shapes from the dough using bell-shaped cutters. Cut as many as possible, then gently press the scraps together, re-roll and cut out more. Lift onto the trays and refrigerate for 15 minutes. Preheat the oven to 160°C (315°F/Gas 2–3). Bake for 20–25 minutes, or until golden underneath. Cool on a wire rack.

Lightly brush the top of some of the biscuits with egg white and lay a piece of gold leaf on top. Rub gently with your finger to transfer the gold leaf from the tissue paper to the biscuit.

NOTE: Edible gold leaf is available from art supply shops and some cake-decorating shops.

Ginger pecan biscotti

MAKES about 20 PREPARATION TIME 30 minutes plus cooling
COOKING TIME 1 hour 20 minutes

100 g (3½ oz/1 cup) pecans
2 eggs
155 g (5½ oz/⅔ cup) soft brown sugar
125 g (4½ oz/1 cup) self-raising flour
90 g (3¼ oz/¾ cup) plain (all-purpose) flour
100 g (3½ oz) glacé (candied) ginger, finely chopped

Preheat the oven to 160°C (315°F/Gas 2–3). Spread the pecans on a baking tray and bake for 10–12 minutes, until fragrant. Tip onto a chopping board to cool, then roughly chop. Cover the baking tray with baking paper.

Beat the eggs and sugar with electric beaters until pale and creamy. Sift the flours into the bowl and then add the nuts and ginger. Mix to a soft dough, then place on the tray and shape into a 9 x 23 cm (3½ x 9 inch) loaf.

Bake for 45 minutes, or until lightly golden. Transfer to a wire rack to cool for about 20 minutes, then carefully cut into 1 cm (½ inch) slices with a large serrated knife. It will be crumbly on the edges, so work slowly and, if possible, try to hold the sides as you cut.

Arrange the slices on baking trays and bake again for about 10 minutes each side. Don't worry if they don't seem fully dry as they will become crisp on cooling. Cool completely before storing in an airtight container.

Blood plum jam

MAKES 2 litres (70 fl oz/8 cups) PREPARATION TIME 20 minutes COOKING TIME 1 hour 15 minutes

25 (2 kg/4 lb 8 oz) medium blood plums
125 ml (4 fl oz/½ cup) lemon juice
1.4 kg (3 lb 2 oz/6½ cups) sugar, warmed

Put two plates in the freezer for testing purposes. Cut the plums in half and remove the pits. Crack a few pits and remove the kernels. Place the kernels in a piece of muslin and tie with string. Place the plums and bag in a large pan and add 1 litre (35 fl oz/4 cups) water. Bring slowly to the boil, then reduce the heat, cover and simmer for 50 minutes, or until the plums have softened.

Add the lemon juice and sugar and stir over low heat, without boiling, for 5 minutes, or until the sugar has dissolved. Bring to the boil and boil for 20 minutes, stirring often. Remove any scum from the surface. When the jam (jelly) falls from a tilted wooden spoon in thick sheets without dripping, start testing for setting point. Remove from the heat, place a little jam on one of the cold plates and place in the freezer for 30 seconds. When setting point is reached, a skin will form on the surface and the jam will wrinkle when pushed. Remove any scum from the surface.

Spoon immediately into clean, warm jars and seal. Turn the jars upside down for 2 minutes, then invert and cool. Label and date. Store in a cool, dark place for 6–12 months. Refrigerate after opening for up to 6 weeks.

Spiced gingerbread

MAKES about 36 PREPARATION TIME 45 minutes
COOKING TIME 10 minutes per batch

- 140 g (5 oz) unsalted butter, softened
- 115 g (4 oz/½ cup) dark brown sugar
- 3 tablespoons treacle
- 1 egg
- 250 g (9 oz/2 cups) plain (all-purpose) flour
- 3 tablespoons self-raising flour
- 3 teaspoons ground ginger
- 2 teaspoons ground cinnamon
- ¾ teaspoon ground cloves
- ¾ teaspoon freshly grated nutmeg
- 1 teaspoon bicarbonate of soda (baking soda)

ICING

- 1 egg white
- ½ teaspoon lemon juice
- 125 g (4½ oz/1 cup) icing (confectioners') sugar, sifted
- assorted food colourings and silver cachous, to decorate

Lightly grease two baking trays. Beat the butter and sugar with electric beaters until light and creamy, then beat in the treacle and egg. Fold in the combined sifted flours, spices and bicarbonate of soda. Turn the dough out onto a lightly floured surface and knead for 2–3 minutes, or until smooth. Cover with plastic wrap and chill for 10 minutes.

Divide the dough in half and roll out between two sheets of baking paper until 4 mm (¼ inch) thick. Place on the trays and chill for 15 minutes. Preheat the oven to 180°C (350°F/Gas 4). Cut out the dough using a 7 cm (2¾ inch) heart-shaped cutter. Using a sharp knife, cut out a 1 cm (½ inch) hole at the top of each shape. Place on the trays and bake for 10 minutes. Stand for 5 minutes before transferring to a wire rack. When the biscuits are cold, decorate with icing.

To make the icing, whisk the egg white until foamy. Add the lemon juice and sugar and stir until glossy. Tint the icing any colour you want, then spoon into paper piping bags. Decorate the gingerbread with the icing and silver cachous. Leave the icing to set.

Lebkuchen

MAKES 35 PREPARATION TIME 25 minutes
COOKING TIME 30 minutes

- 290 g (10¼ oz/2⅓ cups) plain (all-purpose) flour
- 60 g (2¼ oz/½ cup) cornflour (cornstarch)
- 2 teaspoons unsweetened cocoa powder
- 1 teaspoon mixed (pumpkin pie) spice
- 1 teaspoon ground cinnamon
- ½ teaspoon freshly grated nutmeg
- 100 g (3½ oz) unsalted butter, cubed
- 260 g (9¼ oz/¾ cup) golden syrup or dark corn syrup
- 2 tablespoons milk
- 150 g (5½ oz/1 cup) white chocolate melts
- ¼ teaspoon mixed (pumpkin pie) spice, extra, to sprinkle

Preheat the oven to 180°C (350°F/Gas 4). Line two baking trays with baking paper. Sift the flours, cocoa powder and spices into a large bowl and make a well in the centre.

Put the butter, golden syrup and milk in a small saucepan, and stir over low heat until the butter has melted and the mixture is smooth. Add to the dry ingredients. Using a flat-bladed knife, mix with a cutting action until the mixture comes together in small beads. Gather together with your hands and turn out onto a sheet of baking paper.

Roll the dough out to 8 mm (3/8 inch) thick. Cut into heart shapes using a 6 cm (2½ inch) biscuit (cookie) cutter. Place on the trays and bake for 25 minutes, until lightly browned. Leave on the trays to cool slightly before transferring to a wire rack to cool completely.

Place the white chocolate in a small heatproof bowl. Bring a saucepan of water to the boil, then remove from the heat. Sit the bowl of chocolate over the pan, making sure the base of the bowl does not touch the water. Stir occasionally until the chocolate has melted.

Dip one half of each biscuit into the white chocolate and place on a sheet of baking paper until the chocolate has set. Sprinkle the un-iced half of the biscuits with the mixed spice. These biscuits can be stored in an airtight container for up to 5 days.

NOTE: Lebkuchen are a German Christmas treat.

White chocolate lemon truffles

MAKES about 40 PREPARATION TIME 25 minutes plus 4 hours refrigeration COOKING TIME 2 minutes

- 3 tablespoons cream
- 250 g (9 oz) white chocolate melts, chopped
- 1 tablespoon finely grated lemon zest
- 2 teaspoons lemon juice
- 45 g (1½ oz/½ cup) desiccated coconut
- 45 g (1½ oz/¾ cup) toasted shredded coconut

Stir the cream and white chocolate melts in a saucepan over low heat until the chocolate has just melted. Remove the pan from the heat and stir in the lemon zest, lemon juice and the desiccated coconut. Cool, then refrigerate for 1½–2 hours, until firm.

Place teaspoons of the truffle mixture on a foil-lined tray and refrigerate for 2 hours, or until very firm. Roll into balls, then coat with toasted shredded coconut. Keep refrigerated until ready to serve.

Rum truffles

MAKES about 25 PREPARATION TIME 20 minutes plus 50 minutes refrigeration COOKING TIME 1 minute

- 200 g (7 oz) dark cooking chocolate, finely chopped
- 3 tablespoons cream
- 30 g (1 oz) butter
- 50 g (1¾ oz/½ cup) chocolate cake crumbs
- 2 teaspoons dark rum, brandy or whisky
- 95 g (3¼ oz/½ cup) chocolate sprinkles

Line a baking tray with foil. Put the chocolate in a heatproof bowl. Combine the cream and butter in a small pan and stir over low heat until the butter melts and the mixture is just boiling. Pour the hot cream mixture over the chocolate and stir until the chocolate melts and the mixture is smooth.

Stir in the chocolate cake crumbs and rum. Refrigerate for 20 minutes, stirring occasionally, or until firm enough to handle. Roll heaped teaspoons of the mixture into balls.

Spread the chocolate sprinkles on a sheet of greaseproof paper. Roll each truffle in sprinkles, then place on the baking tray. Refrigerate for 30 minutes, or until firm. Serve in small paper patty cups, if desired.

NOTE: Truffles can also be rolled in dark cocoa powder. They can be made up to a week in advance and refrigerated in an airtight container.

Mini fruit truffle puddings

MAKES about 44 PREPARATION TIME 40 minutes COOKING TIME nil

- 500 g (1 lb 2 oz) fruit cake
- 2 tablespoons desiccated coconut
- 80 ml (2½ fl oz/⅓ cup) dark rum
- 30 g (1 oz/⅓ cup) flaked almonds, toasted and crushed
- 400 g (14 oz) dark chocolate buttons, melted
- 2 teaspoons oil
- 150 g (5½ oz) white chocolate, melted
- 1 stick of angelica (see Note)
- 8 red glacé (candied) cherries

Finely chop the fruit cake in a food processor. Combine in a bowl with the coconut, rum, almonds and 150 g (5½ oz) of the melted dark chocolate buttons and mix thoroughly. Roll two teaspoons of the mixture at a time into balls and place on a baking tray covered with baking paper.

Place the remaining melted dark chocolate buttons and oil in a small bowl and stir well. Sit each truffle on a fork and dip in the chocolate to coat. Carefully remove, allowing any excess to drain away. Place back on the paper and leave to set. Do not refrigerate.

When the chocolate has set, spoon the white chocolate into a small piping (icing) bag fitted with a small nozzle (or use a plastic bag and snip off a small corner) and drizzle chocolate on top of each pudding (to look like custard). Decorate the tops of the puddings with small pieces of angelica and cherry before the chocolate sets.

NOTE: Angelica is the candied stems or leaf ribs of a tall parsley-like plant.

White cake truffles

MAKES about 25 PREPARATION TIME 25 minutes
COOKING TIME 5 minutes

250 g (9 oz) Madeira cake crumbs
2 tablespoons chopped glacé (candied) orange peel
1 tablespoon apricot jam (jelly)
2 tablespoons cream
100 g (3½ oz) white chocolate, melted
edible gold leaf, to decorate

CHOCOLATE COATING
150 g (5½ oz) white chocolate, chopped
20 g (¾ oz) Copha (white vegetable shortening), chopped

Line a baking tray with foil. Combine the cake crumbs with the chopped peel, jam, cream and melted white chocolate. Mix until smooth, then roll into balls using 2 teaspoons of mixture for each ball.

To make the chocolate coating, combine the chocolate and Copha in a heatproof bowl. Bring a saucepan of water to the boil, then remove from the heat and sit the bowl over the pan, making sure the bowl does not touch the water. Stir until the chocolate and the shortening have melted. Dip the truffles into the chocolate, wipe the excess on the edge of the bowl and leave them to set on the tray. Decorate with gold leaf.

Pecan shortbread butter bursts

MAKES 42 PREPARATION TIME 30 minutes
COOKING TIME 10 minutes

175 g (6 oz) butter, softened
115 g (4 oz/½ cup) caster (superfine) sugar
1 teaspoon natural vanilla extract
125 g (4½ oz/1 cup) plain (all-purpose) flour
3 tablespoons rice flour
90 g (3¼ oz/¾ cup) toasted pecans, finely chopped
125 g (4½ oz/1 cup) icing (confectioners') sugar, sifted, for dusting

Preheat the oven to 180°C (350°F/Gas 4). Line two baking trays with baking paper. Beat the butter, caster sugar and vanilla with electric beaters until pale and fluffy. Sift in the flours, add the pecans and stir until well combined.

Roll 2 teaspoons of the mixture into balls and place on the trays, allowing room for spreading. Bake for 10 minutes, or until lightly browned. Allow to cool on the trays for 2 minutes. Dust with half the icing sugar while still hot, then cool on wire racks. Dust with the remaining icing sugar before serving.

Crackle cookies

MAKES about 60 PREPARATION TIME 20 minutes plus 3 hours refrigeration COOKING TIME 25 minutes per tray

- 125 g (4½ oz) unsalted butter, softened
- 370 g (13 oz/2 cups) soft brown sugar
- 1 teaspoon natural vanilla extract
- 2 eggs
- 60 g (2¼ oz) dark chocolate, melted
- 80 ml (2½ fl oz/⅓ cup) milk
- 340 g (12 oz/2¾ cups) plain (all-purpose) flour
- 2 tablespoons unsweetened cocoa powder
- 2 teaspoons baking powder
- ¼ teaspoon ground allspice
- 85 g (3 oz/⅔ cup) chopped pecans
- icing (confectioners') sugar, to coat

Beat the butter, sugar and vanilla until light and creamy. Beat in the eggs, one at a time. Stir in the chocolate and milk. Sift the flour, cocoa, baking powder, allspice and a pinch of salt into the butter mixture and mix well. Stir in the pecans, then refrigerate for at least 3 hours, or overnight.

Preheat the oven to 180°C (350°F/Gas 4). Roll tablespoons of the mixture into balls and roll in sifted icing sugar. Place the cookies well apart on two greased baking trays. Bake for 20–25 minutes, until lightly browned. Cool on a wire rack.

Chocolate clusters

MAKES about 40 PREPARATION TIME 35 minutes COOKING TIME nil

- 125 g (4½ oz) dark chocolate melts
- 125 g (4½ oz) white chocolate melts
- 125 g (4½ oz/⅔ cup) dried mixed fruit
- 125 g (4½ oz) glacé (candied) ginger, chopped
- 30 g (1 oz) dark chocolate melts, extra, melted
- 30 g (1 oz) white chocolate melts, extra, melted

Put the dark chocolate in a heatproof bowl. Bring a saucepan of water to the boil, then remove from the heat. Sit the bowl over the pan, making sure the bowl does not touch the water. Stir occasionally until the chocolate has melted. Cool slightly. Repeat with the white chocolate.

Stir the mixed fruit into the dark chocolate. Stir the ginger into the white chocolate. Drop spoonfuls of the mixtures onto foil-lined trays, and leave to set at room temperature. Drizzle with the extra melted chocolate.

Index

Published in 2011 by Murdoch Books Pty Limited

Murdoch Books Australia
Pier 8/9
23 Hickson Road
Millers Point NSW 2000
Phone: +61 (0) 2 8220 2000
Fax: +61 (0) 2 8220 2558
www.murdochbooks.com.au

Murdoch Books UK Limited
Erico House, 6th Floor
93–99 Upper Richmond Road
Putney, London SW15 2TG
Phone: +44 (0) 20 8785 5995
Fax: +44 (0) 20 8785 5985
www.murdochbooks.co.uk

Publisher: Lynn Lewis
Designer: Susanne Geppert
Design concept: Heather Menzies
Cover design: Susanne Geppert
Project editor: Justine Harding
Project manager: Liz Malcolm
Editorial assistant: Kit Carstairs
Production: Renee Melbourne
Incidental photography and styling: Stuart Scott, Jane Hann, Alan Benson, Louise Bickle

National Library of Australia Cataloguing-in-Publication entry

Title: Celebrate christmas : a bumper collection of traditional
recipes and festive craft projects.
ISBN: 9781742667188 (pbk.)
Notes: Includes index.
Subjects: Christmas.
Christmas cooking.
Christmas decorations
Handicraft.
Dewey Number: 394.268282
A catalogue record for this book is available from the British Library.

Printed by 1010 Printing International Ltd in 2011
PRINTED IN CHINA.

IMPORTANT: Those who might be at risk from the effects of salmonella poisoning (the elderly, pregnant women, young children and those suffering from immune deficiency diseases) should consult their doctor with any concerns about eating raw eggs.

OVEN GUIDE: You may find cooking times vary depending on the oven you are using. For fan-forced ovens, as a general rule, set the oven temperature to 20°C (35°F) lower than indicated in the recipe.